TOTALACTION

This book is part of the **Goodyear Series in Education**, Professor Theodore W. Hipple, Editor. University of Florida, Gainesville.

OTHER GOODYEAR BOOKS IN LANGUAGE ARTS & READING

DO YOU READ ME? *Practical Approaches to Teaching Reading Comprehension*
Arnold A. Griese

I CAN MAKE IT ON MY OWN *Functional Reading Ideas and Activities for Daily Survival*
Michelle Berman and Linda Shevitz

IMAGINE THAT! *Illustrated Poems and Creative Learning Experiences*
Joyce King and Carol Katzman

THE LANGUAGE ARTS IDEA BOOK *Classroom Activities for Children*
Joanne Schaff

MAINSTREAMING LANGUAGE ARTS AND SOCIAL STUDIES *Special Ideas and Activities for the Whole Class*
Anne H. Adams, Charles R. Coble, Paul B. Hounshell

MAKING KIDS CLICK *Independent Activities in Reading and the Language Arts*
Linda Polon and Aileen Cantwell

NEW DIMENSIONS IN ENGLISH *An Ideabook of Language Arts Activities for Middle and Secondary School Teachers*
Joanne Schaff

AN OUNCE OF PREVENTION PLUS A POUND OF CURE *Tests and Techniques for Aiding Individual Readers*
Ronald W. Bruton

PHORGAN'S PHONICS
Harry W. Forgan

THE READING CORNER *Ideas, Games, and Activities for Individualizing Reading*
Harry W. Forgan

SUCCESS IN BEGINNING READING AND WRITING *The Basal Concept of the Future*
Anne H. Adams

READING FOR SURVIVAL IN TODAY'S SOCIETY *Volumes I and II*
Anne H. Adams, Anne Flowers, Elsa E. Woods

WRITE UP A STORM *Creative Writing Ideas and Activities for the Middle Grades*
Linda Polon and Aileen Cantwell

THE WRITING CORNER
Arnold Cheyney

For information about these, or Goodyear books in Science, Math, Social Studies, General Methods, and Centers, write to

Janet Jackson
Goodyear Publishing Company
1640 Fifth Street
Santa Monica, CA 90401
(213) 393-6731

TOTALACTION

Ideas and Activities for
Teaching Children
Ages Five to Eight

Pat Short
Billee Davidson

GOODYEAR
Publishing Company, Inc.
Santa Monica, California

Short, Pat.
  Totalaction: ideas and activities for teaching children ages
five to eight.

  (Goodyear series in education)
  1. Education, Primary—Curricula—Handbooks, manuals, etc.
2. Creative activities and seat work—Handbooks, manuals, etc.
I. Davidson, Billee, joint author. II. Title.
LB1523.S57   372.1'1'02   79-17086
ISBN 0-87620-902-9

Y-9029-3

ISBN: 0-87620-902-9

Cover and text designer: Mike Yazzolino
Production editor: Pam Tully
Compositor: Project Publishing & Design, Inc.

Current printing (last digit):
10 9 8 7 6 5 4 3 2

Printed in the United States of America

For young children with their free spirits and active curiosity.

And to our children, Leslie and Samantha, and our husbands, Ian and David, with our thanks for their patience and encouragement.

CONTENTS

PREFACE ix

INTRODUCTION x

COLORS, SHAPES, AND SIZES 1

Skills 2

Vocabulary 2

Color Names 2
Line Names 2
Shape Names 2
Solid Shape Names 2
Pattern Names 2
Surface Texture Words 2
Size Names 2
Number Names 2
Computational Names 2
Metric Terms 2

Workcard Sets 3

Which One Is Different? 3
Tangrams 3
Complete-a-Shape 3
Match-a-Pattern 4
Matching Color Blocks 5
Matching Shapes and Bead Patterns 5
Pattern Cards 5
Matching Words and Colors 6
Barney Beagle 6
Read, Print, and Draw 7
Three Things 7
Counting 8
Balance 9
Points, Edges, and Surfaces 9
Tell How These Are Alike 10
What Is _____? 11
Mr. Meter 11
Making Sets 12
One-to-One Correspondence 12
Number Know-how 12

Shape-a-Pattern 12
Imaginative Thought 13
Line Drawings 14

Graphs 15

Graphing Ideas 15
Types of Graphs 15

Booklets 16

Games And Tasks 17

Color Memory Game 17
Reading Readiness Task 17
Shape or Color Boards 17
Sorting Tasks 18
Pentagon 18
Venn Diagrams 19
Shape Chase 19
Domino Shapes 20
Sequencing Shapes or Colors 20
Line-a-Shape 20
Mystery Mittens 21
Word Worms 21
Help Me Color This 22
Mysterious Shapes 23
Arithmetic Flags 23
Missing Shape Game 23
Shape-O 23
Color-O 24

Projects 24

Construction 24
Collections 25
Color Days 25
Finding Shapes and Lines 26
Mobiles 26

Handwork 27

Cut and Paste 27
Paper Tearing 27

Experimenting with Color	27
Collages	28
Texture Paintings	28
Concentric Shapes	28

Physical Activities   29

Movements	29
Pyramids	29
Shape and Line Maze	30
Equipment Maze	30

Worksheets   31

Count and Color	32
Fill-ins	33
Shape Train Scramble	38
Tangram Patterns	40
Three Things	41
Cut and Paste	42
Think and Draw	43
Line Drawings	44
Sort-a-Word	47
Box Patterns	48

CIRCUS SIGHTS AND SOUNDS   51

Skills   52

Vocabulary   52

Animal Names	52
Performer Names	52
Equipment Names	52
Sensory and Descriptive Words	52
Skill Words	52

Workcard Sets   53

What's Missing?	53
Popcorn Poof! Ideas to Promote Creative Speaking and Writing	53
Make a Set	55
Feet, Feet, Feet!	55
If	57
Big Bonnie	57
Balancing	58
Sights and Sounds	59

Graphs   61

Graphing Ideas	61
Types of Graphs	61

Booklets   62

Child-made Booklets	62
Class-made Booklets	62

Games and Tasks   63

Come to the Circus	63
Missing Animals or Clowns	63
Balloon Man	64
Pin the Nose on the Clown	64

Tent Toss	65
Concentration	66
Greater Than, Less Than, Equal To	66
Money Makers	67
Climbing High	67
Leopold Lion	68
Elephants Walk in Circus Rings	68
Sorting Carts	69
Concession	69
Cracking the Whip	70
Sound Cans	70
Sound Discrimination	70
Venn Diagrams	71

Projects   71

Posters and Advertising	71
Circus Day	72
Models, Dioramas, and Construction	72
Concession Stand	73
Puppets	74
Research	75
Mobiles	76

Handwork   77

Clown Hats	77
Plasticene, Clay-Dough, or Clay Animals	77
Finger Painting	78
"C" Animals	78
Balloon Heads	78
Configuration Animals	79
Stand-up Animals	79
Paper Strip Clown	79
Be a Clown!	80
Paper Bag or Box Animals	80
Beasts	80

Physical Activities   81

Hoops	81
Ropes	81
Balance Beam or Bench	81
Trampoline	81
Tumbling	81
Rhythm Balls	81
Movement to Music	82
Movement Instructions	82

Worksheets   82

Fill-ins	83
Arithmetic or Phonetic Fill-in	84
Finish Me	85
Configurations	86
Who's Balancing This Ball?	87
Find Sixteen Hidden Letters	88
Cut and Paste	89
Big Bonnie	90
Make a Set	91

WATER, WATER, EVERYWHERE 93
Skills 94
Vocabulary 94
  Bodies of Water 94
  Land Affected by Water 94
  Water in Motion 94
  Boats 94
  Navigation Terms 94
  Common Parts of a Boat 94
  Fish 94
  Water Life 95
  Man-made Structures Associated
    With Water 95
Workcard Sets 95
  Nautical Notes 95
  Anchors Aweigh 96
  If 97
  Parts of the Whole 97
  Story Starters 98
  Thought Waves 98
  Sounders 99
  Versus 100
  Sea Scramble 100
Booklets 102
  Child-made Booklets 102
  Class-made Booklets 103
Games And Tasks 104
  Matching Tasks 104
  Ordering Tasks 106
  Directional Tasks 107
  Floating Pictures 108
  Fishing Fun 108
  Ships' Logs 109
  Water in Motion 110
  List-a-Fish 110
  Fish Bowl 111
  Ship Ahoy! 112
  Water Works 113
  Compound Words 114
  Treasure Hunt 115
  Row, Row, Row Your Boat 116

Projects 116
  Things That Dissolve and Change
    in Water 116
  Float or Sink 117
  Bridge Construction 117
  Aquariums 118
  Research 118
  Driftwood 119
  Things You Can Do With
    Seashells 119
  Photographic Analysis 120
Handwork 121
  Wax and Tissue 121
  Paper Plate Aquariums 121
  Paper Strip Creatures 122
  Fish 124
  Boats 125
  Clay or Clay-Dough Sea Creatures 127
  Stick or Balsa Rafts 128
  Hole Punch Fish 128
  Plasticene Wash Pictures 128
  Wax Resists 128
Physical Activities 129
  Bridges 129
  Water Orientation 129
Worksheets 130
  Fill-ins 131
  Sailing, Sailing 133
  Boats 134
  What Am I? 135
  Above, Below 136
  Seashells 137
  The Fisherman 138
  Fish 139
  Dot-to-Dot 140
  Anchors Aweigh 141
  Maze 142
  Crossword Puzzle 143

PREFACE

Totalaction is not a curriculum guide. It is a resource of ideas and activities revolving around a thematic approach. It is intended to provide a stimulus for teachers to combine their own ideas with the ideas presented here into an effective program for young children between the ages of five and eight.

The activities and suggestions in *Totalaction* have been successfully, and have been received enthusiastically by both children and teachers. We hope that our ideas will be helpful for those of you who want to improve basic skills and to develop further the total growth of each child.

The depth and scope to which the themes in this book can be developed is dependent upon the ability, interest, and age of each child. Every child can, however, gain a basic understanding of the skills contained within each thematic unit. Combining the activities and ideas presented here with your own teaching style and resources will help you motivate each child to work to capacity level.

INTRODUCTION

Totalaction implies both mental and physical activity. An active learner is one who participates, explores, and develops through actual and vicarious experiences. An effective program stimulates the learner's interest and motivates him to activity. This book provides a variety of suggestions and ideas for you, the teacher, to nurture this activity, while fulfilling the needs of your students.

Totalaction suggests the organization of parts into a whole. In considering the whole child and the total growth of that child, the teacher must recognize and be sensitive to individual interests, experiences, and rates of development. This book allows for learner differences by presenting a wide range of materials for you to draw upon. You can select activities that will challenge each child at his or her own level of achievement.

Totalaction emphasizes the thematic approach—the organization of the entire curriculum under one theme. Within each thematic unit there is great flexibility to allow for individual teaching styles, strengths, and resources, as well as learner interests and abilities. The materials in this book may be presented in traditional group lessons, at work stations, as part of an integrated day, or in interest centers. At the core of each thematic unit are the basic skills which will, to a varying degree, be mastered by each child. The subject areas—language arts, arithmetic, science, social studies, fine arts, and physical education—and the skills drawn from this curriculum are woven together by the central theme. It is this theme which lends a common basis and emphasis to the diversity of subject areas and skills.

The three thematic units in *Totalaction*—Colors, Shapes, and Sizes; Circus Sights and Sounds; and Water, Water, Everywhere—present a multitude of WORKCARD SETS, GRAPHS, BOOKLETS, GAMES AND TASKS, PROJECTS, HANDWORK, PHYSICAL ACTIVITIES, and WORKSHEETS. We feel that for education to be meaningful, teachers must consider a wide range of experiences and abilities in order to develop a comprehensive program aimed at reaching each child. Our intent is not that each child master, or even attempt, every activity in *Totalaction*. Our intent is to provide enough alternatives for you to choose from.

VOCABULARY

The VOCABULARY lists at the beginning of each thematic unit aid you in preparing your own materials and in guiding the development of the children's vocabularies. The lists were developed to span kindergarten through grade three and, thus, you may view some of the VOCABULARY as being too difficult, or too easy for your pupils. You can choose from or extend the VOCABULARY lists in order to suit the abilities of the children or expand their oral and written vocabularies.

WORKCARD SETS

Sets of workcards in each thematic unit cover the ability range of five to eight-year-olds and to appeal to a variety of needs and interests. The WORKCARD SETS are designed to cover all areas of the curriculum and aid you in teaching and in reinforcing the skills listed at the beginning of each thematic unit. All the WORKCARD SETS, as with the other activities in *Totalaction*, are simply ideas for you to extend and adapt to fit your needs and the needs of your students.

The WORKCARD SETS were used most successfully in our multiaged primary (kindergarten through grade three) classrooms. But we did not create or use the WORKCARD SETS as class assignments. Every child would not necessarily complete each card in each set. Every child, whether in kindergarten or grade three, would be individually assigned or guided to choose workcards geared to his or her need and ability. We did, however, make certain that the entire class understood the procedures for completing the cards in each of the sets.

GRAPHS

Since we feel that understanding is increased when primary children visually record what they experience, graphing ideas are included in each thematic unit. We used picture, bar, line, matching, and set graphs to pictorially represent what was seen or done. GRAPHS may be completed by the entire class, by small groups, or by individual students. GRAPHS should preferably be large and be kept within easy access for referral by pupils. Written records or captions might accompany the GRAPHS and could be done by older students.

Again, these are simply graphing ideas. You may have terrific graphing opportunities arise spontaneously during class discussions, outings, or other activities. Capitalize on them—they can be wonderful learning experiences for you and the children.

BOOKLETS

BOOKLETS can serve as a means of recording experiences or as a vehicle for creative expression. They can be undertaken as class or individual activities. They may consist of simply pictures, pictures and captions, or stories. You can print dictated captions or short stories in the BOOKLETS of children who cannot yet read or write. And you may be surprised at their ability to "read" (by recall) their statements to you.

GAMES AND TASKS

As with the WORKCARD SETS, the GAMES AND TASKS are suggested activities for reinforcing the skills stated for each thematic unit. Every child may not need, enjoy, or become proficient at each activity in these sections. It is for the teacher and the student to mutually decide which GAMES AND TASKS will positively benefit the individual.

PROJECTS

Within the three thematic units, the PROJECTS take a variety of forms. Generally, activities related to constructing, collecting, observing, discovering, and researching are dealt with in these sections. All of these activities would require time, interaction, and guidance to complete. Individuality and creativity should be stressed. Not all children will undertake each project, nor will all children reach similar outcomes from their explorations.

HANDWORK

HANDWORK is, most simply, work done by the hands. These suggested activities are related to the development of fine motor skills and creative expression through art. Each child should be given the opportunity to explore with and express himself through a wide variety of mediums.

PHYSICAL ACTIVITIES

PHYSICAL ACTIVITIES can take place in the classroom, gymnasium, school grounds, local park, or community center. They may occur anywhere you and the children feel comfortable in your exploration of physical movement, space, and equipment. You may work with a whole class, a group of children, or an individual child to promote motor skills and growth.

WORKSHEETS

The WORKSHEETS enhance and expand the other activities within each thematic unit. They are ready for you to tear out, duplicate, and use as you see fit within your classroom.

TOTALACTION

VOCABULARY
Color Names
Line Names
Shape Names
Solid Shape Names
Pattern Names
Surface Texture Words
Size Names
Number Names
Computational Names
Metric Terms

WORKCARD SETS
Which One Is Different?
Tangrams
Complete-a-Shape
Match-a-Pattern
Matching Color Blocks
Matching Shapes and Bead
   Patterns
Pattern Cards
Matching Words and Colors
Barney Beagle
Read, Print, and Draw
Three Things
Counting
Balance
Points, Edges, Surfaces
Tell How These Are Alike
What Is?
Mr. Meter
Making Sets
One-to-One Correspondence
Number Know-how

Shape-a-Pattern
Imaginative Thought
Line Drawings

BOOKLETS

GRAPHS
Graphing Ideas
Types of Graphs

COLORS, SHAPES, AND SIZES

GAMES AND TASKS
Color Memory Game
Reading Readiness Task
Shape or Color Boards
Sorting Tasks
Pentagon
Venn Diagrams
Shape Chase
Domino Shapes
Sequencing Shapes or Colors
Line-a-Shape
Mystery Mittens
Word Worms
Help Me Color This
Mysterious Shapes
Arithmetic Flags
Missing Shape Game
Shape-O
Color-O

PROJECTS
Construction
Collections
Color Days
Finding Shapes and Lines
Mobiles

HANDWORK
Cut and Paste
Paper Tearing
Experimenting With Color
Collages
Texture Paintings
Concentric Shapes

PHYSICAL ACTIVITIES
Movements
Pyramids
Shape and Line Maze
Equipment Maze

WORKSHEETS
Count and Color
Fill-ins
Shape Train Scramble
Tangram Patterns
Three Things
Cut and Paste
Think and Draw
Line Drawings
Sort-a-Word
Box Patterns

SKILLS

The core and basis of this thematic unit is the development of the following skills:

recognition and understanding of the unit vocabulary

classification of lines, shapes, patterns, textures, and sizes

utilization of lines, shapes, and patterns in construction, handwork, and drawing

comparison of shapes, sizes, patterns, and textures

visual discrimination of colors, shapes, sizes, and patterns

tactile discrimination of textures, shapes, and sizes

interpretation and investigation of the units of measure

interpretation of oral and written directions

awareness of numbers, ordinals, and comparison terms

knowledge, interpretation, and creation of graphs

expansion of verbal and nonverbal creative expression

development of recall skills

growth of fine motor skills

reinforcement of basic number facts

reinforcement of phonetic sounds

VOCABULARY

Color Names
red, blue, yellow, green, orange, purple, brown, black, white, gray, pink

Line Names
wavy, straight, curved, zigzag, intersecting, parallel, horizontal, perpendicular

Shape Names
circle, square, right triangle, equilateral triangle, rectangle, oval, pentagon, hexagon, diamond, semicircle, octagon, rhombus, trapezoid, parallelogram

Solid Shape Names
cube, cone, cylinder, sphere, pyramid, tetrahedron, prism

Pattern Names
polka dot, paisley, stripes, solid, plaid, tartan, check, herringbone, hound's tooth, abstract

Surface Texture Words
rough, smooth, shiny, dull, hard, soft, bumpy, uneven, even, flat, curved

Size Names
large, big, bigger, biggest, huge, enormous, greater than, less than, small, smaller, smallest, little, tiny, thick, thin, wide, narrow, long, short, medium, most, least, few, more, between

Number Names
zero to one hundred, fractions (quarter, third, half)

Computational Names
add, plus, minus, take away, subtract, equal, set, multiply, divide, groups, borrow, carry

Metric Terms
meter, centimeter, millimeter, centicube, liter, gram

WORKCARD SETS

Which One Is Different?
The teacher makes simple cards which show two or three like objects and one object which differs in some way.

The child chooses or is given a few cards and orally denotes the differences and similarities.

If the child is working independently, he or she could place a block or peg on top of the object that is different and leave the cards for the teacher to check.

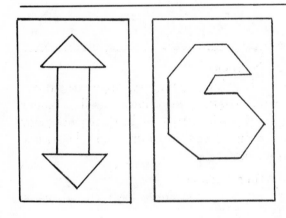

Tangrams
These workcards are made by placing tangram pieces in various patterns on colored cardboard and tracing around each individual piece or around the outline of the entire figure.

The seven tangram pieces, duplicated from the WORKSHEETS, can be made from heavy cardboard or wood and include one square, two large triangles, one medium triangle, two small triangles, and one parallelogram.

The children copy the patterns by placing tangram pieces on top of the workcards or they trace the tangram pieces to make their own patterns.

Complete-a-Shape
These are self-correcting puzzles.

The teacher makes many small puzzles by drawing or tracing shapes on colored cardboard and printing the shape names on the fronts or backs.

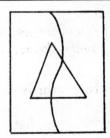

3

The puzzles are then cut in two with wavy, zigzag, or straight lines.

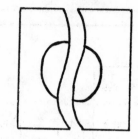

Small workcards, such as the shape puzzles, can be made from colored paper scraps. Paper scraps of various colors, weights, and sizes are often available free of charge from your school board offices or local printing companies.

Match-a-Pattern
Fabric, wallpaper, and magazine pictures with patterns such as plaid or polka dot are mounted onto pairs of cards for matching and sorting into a labeled sorting box.

Magnetic rubber tape adds fun to matching activities. Strips of this adhesive tape can be purchased at teacher stores and can be cut into small pieces to be attached to the back of workcards, pictures, and cutouts. Children may then carry out their matching and sorting activities on any magnetic surface — the side of a filing cabinet, a magnetic chalkboard, a metal heating tray, or a stainless steel serving tray.

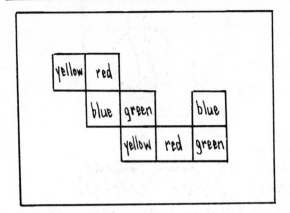

Matching Color Blocks

When making these workcards, use colored squares of the same dimension as the cubed blocks you have available.

The child places blocks on top of the card to copy the pattern.

With experience, the child could look at the card and repeat the pattern elsewhere or create patterns of his or her own for classmates to copy.

Matching Shapes and Bead Patterns

The child looks at the teacher-made card and repeats the given pattern using shape blocks or colored beads.

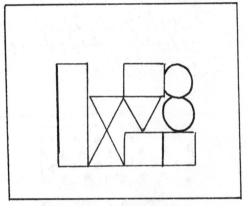

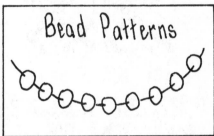

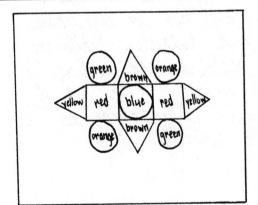

Pattern Cards

The child is given a colored pattern card and a matching pattern on a duplicated worksheet.

The child colors the worksheet according to the pattern card.

Matching Words and Colors

Draw the clowns and mount paper clips above each head.

Add a paper pocket to hold the construction paper hats.

The child chooses and clips on the colored hat which corresponds to the word on the clown's collar.

Shapes or numbers may be used in the same way.

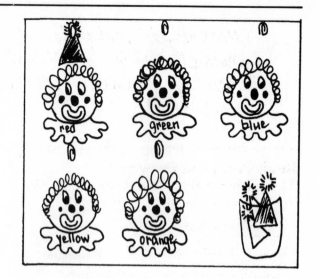

Barney Beagle

This set of cards could include all of the unit vocabulary.

As the child progresses in skill, words could be substituted for the pictures on the cards.

The child would read and make a picture for each of the statements on the card.

Maybe you'd like to "say" something to your students. Keep a small notepad (with an inscription such as, Mrs. Davidson says:) handy for writing special notes to individual children. The notes can be placed on children's desks, or pasted or paperclipped in their notebooks asking that a certain book be read, workcard be completed, game be played, or conference be held.

Personalized notepads can be made by adding inscriptions to purchased notepaper or by placing designs and words onto colored newsprint.

Read, Print, and Draw

The teacher makes a set of workcards with interpretive statements, such as:

a necklace with twenty round beads

a train with seven rectangular cars

a garden with eight yellow flowers

this goes round and round

the school is built of brown bricks

a man with round and oval balloons

the star is made of triangles

a house with five square windows

this is long and thin

this has spots

the last car is green

the middle light is yellow

the tallest boy has fuzzy brown hair

a castle with two arches and three oval windows

a girl in a plaid dress

The child chooses or is given a card and reads, prints, and illustrates the statement.

The teacher may also wish to provide blank "Read, Print, and Draw" cards on which a child may print his or her own statement for another classmate to follow.

Three Things

These workcards are for identifying sets of three things, and may include:

three kinds of shapes

three kinds of lines

three things that are round

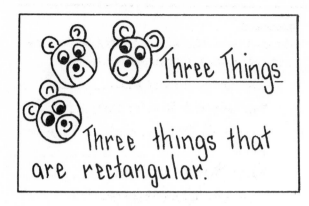

Three Things

Three things that are rectangular.

three things that are square

three things that are short

three things that are red

three yellow vegetables

three red fruits

three things that are huge

three things with round parts

three things that are heavy

three things that are smooth

three things that are striped

A corresponding mimeo could be made on which the child can illustrate his or her workcard (see WORKSHEETS, page 41).

How do you organize and display your workcards and matching worksheets? With bent bookends! Claim any discarded bookends from remodeled libraries — the bases can be bent up by hammering or by exerting steady pressure on them. Worksheets may then be placed on a counter or shelf and the bookend, which can now hold your workcards, may stand on top. Bookends can be painted, covered with decorative adhesive vinyl, or have directional signs attached.

Counting

Simple, teacher-made cards such as this develop shape recognition, perception, and counting ability.

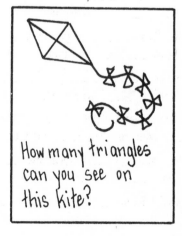

How many circles can you see in this picture?

How many triangles can you see on this kite?

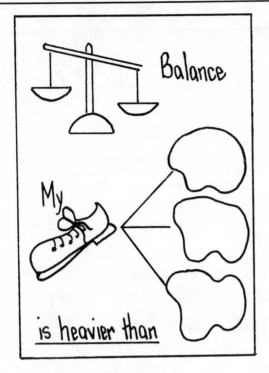

Balance

According to the materials available, make a set of balance workcards, such as:

My shoe is heavier than _____.

My sweater is heavier than _____.

_____ is heavier than a large red block.

My book is heavier than _____.

_____ is lighter than the doll.

A chalkboard eraser is lighter than _____.

Two pieces of chalk are lighter than _____.

Three nails balance _____.

Five dog biscuits balance _____.

Instruct the children to determine the information asked for, by placing the various objects on a purchased or simple homemade balance.

Printed or drawn answers could be recorded in a notebook or the actual objects could be placed directly on the workcard.

Points, Edges, and Surfaces

These workcards are to be used with wooden, plastic, or cardboard models.

Make a workcard for each object, perhaps including a picture.

A prism has _____ points, _____ edges, and _____ surfaces.

A cone has _____ points, _____ edges, and _____ surfaces.

A cylinder has _____ points, _____ edges, and _____ surfaces.

A tetrahedron has _____ points, _____ edges, and _____ surfaces.

A cube has _____ points, _____ edges, and _____ surfaces

A pyramid has _____ points, _____ edges, and _____ surfaces.

A sphere has _____ points, _____ edges, and _____ surfaces.

Tell How These Are Alike

Given a workcard, the child describes orally or in written sentences the similarities of designated objects, such as:

a window and a door

a button and a doorknob

a pie and a doughnut

a salami and a candy stick

an orange and a ball

a piece of pipe and a toilet tissue roll

Laminating is a must! Protect your workcards and greatly increase their lifespan by covering them, front and back, with laminating film. Schools or school districts sometimes offer laminating film in supply requisitions or on a pupil-ratio system. Laminating machines can be found in universities, school board offices, teacher centers, or individual schools.

If laminating film or machines are not available in your district, contact a bookbinder ~ film can be purchased in rolls of varying lengths, widths, and costs. This film can be easily ironed onto your workcards by setting the iron at a low heat. Several cards may be placed on the film, another piece of film placed on top, and the layers ironed together. (Keep a straight pin handy to puncture any bubbles.) Trim around each card leaving a small edging of film to seal in the card.

The initial cost and effort will be well rewarded by preserving your work and saving hours of repairing and remaking.

What Is _____?

Make a workcard for each adjective you wish to teach; for example, brown, red, blue, colorful, round, square, oval, fat, thin, tall, flat, small, spotted, striped, checked, shiny, hard, rough, smooth, straight, curved, or wavy.

Some children may print one sentence, while others may print ten, or even twenty.

Examples of children's sentences are:

> An elephant is big.
>
> A house is big.
>
> A fir tree is big.
>
> A skyscraper is big.

Mr. Meter

Teachers make cards to reflect their equipment resources, and may include instructions, such as:

> "Measure the table. Use a red centimeter cube."
>
> "Measure the length of the carpet. Use a large rectangular block."
>
> "Measure how long the room is. Use a large square block and a large rectangular block. Which shape did you need the most of? Draw a graph to show what you did."
>
> "List all the square things you could use to measure the teacher's desk."
>
> "Measure how wide the door is. Use a library book. What shape is the door? What shape is the book?"
>
> "Measure how high the piano bench is. Use green blocks."
>
> "Measure how high the chalkboard is from the floor. Use a chalkboard eraser. What shape is the eraser?"
>
> "Measure how high the garbage can is. Use yellow blocks."
>
> "Measure the hall. Use a meter stick."

Making Sets

Pairs of workcards are made, one with a picture and the other with a description of the set.

The child takes the entire set of workcards and reads and matches the pairs.

a set of 3 triangles

One-to-One Correspondence

Done similarly to the previous set, the child matches cards having large and small shapes.

Draw 6 circles.

Color the 1st and 4th circles.

Draw 10 oval balloons.
Number them.
Color balloons five, three, nine, eight, and two.

Number Know-how

Numbers, number words, or ordinals can be used.

The children follow the directions given on each card.

Shape-a-Pattern

The teacher suggests one, two, or more shapes to use as the basis for a pattern or a picture of such things as a clown, a kite, a giraffe, a horse, a train, a fish, a boy, a snowman, a house, a truck, an owl, or a cat.

Shape-a-Pattern

Make a house with ▯s, ▢s.

12

The child chooses a card and completes the task by drawing the picture or pattern using only the shapes suggested on the workcard.

A young child may trace around various sizes of cardboard or plastic shapes as an aid to completing the assignment.

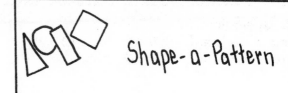

Shape-a-Pattern

Make an owl with Os.

Teacher or child-made boxes of heavy cardboard are excellent for storing and displaying your workcards. The boxes can be made in assorted sizes to accommodate your various workcards. They can be spray painted, decorated by the children, covered with colored adhesive vinyl, or covered with wallpaper scraps.

For some box patterns see Worksheets, pages 48 and 49.

Imaginative Thought

This set of workcards would be made to promote thinking for discussion or story-writing activities:

What might happen if we didn't have squares?

How would the world be different if there were no circles?

What would it be like without colors?

Why do we need the color green?

What might happen if everything turned orange at night?

What would it be like if the only shape was the triangle?

What would happen if you could only walk in a zigzag line?

What if trees grew horizontally instead of perpendicular to the ground?

What if everything you touched felt prickly?

What if everything alive had purple stripes?

Children should be encouraged to and will enjoy creating their own thought-provoking questions for class discussion.

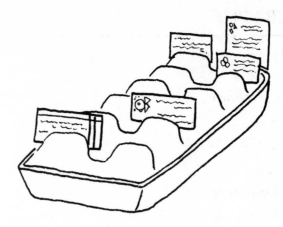

Inverted egg cartons with a slit in each section allow for easy display of small workcards and selection by pupils.

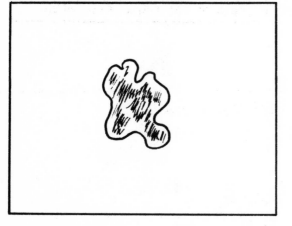

Line Drawings

The child is given a piece of paper with any line or shape, or even a hole in it.

The child turns his or her paper in any position to draw a picture incorporating the teacher-made figure.

This may be a workcard or a worksheet.

See WORKSHEETS, pages 44, 45, 46.

GRAPHS

Graphing Ideas

favorite colors

shape of face

size of feet

size of hands

heights

color of hair

color of eyes

color of clothes on a given day

shapes in the room

textures

fruit or vegetable colors

color of cars in an intersection

number of cars passing in a set time

color of houses in a block

patterns on clothing

color of shoes

Colors of Cars

red □□□□

blue □□□□□

yellow □□□

green □

black □□□□□□

brown □□□□

We saw 24 cars.
Most of the cars were black.

Our Hair Color

blond Robert Jeff

black Joey Lynda Johnny Mary

brown Tracey Gary Leslie

red Billy Julie Helen David Melanie

Types of Graphs

picture

bar

line

matching

set graphs

Some ideas for booklets are:

    things that are red

    things small to a mouse

    things big to a bear

    things that are round

    things that are smooth

    things longer than one meter

    things shorter than one centimeter

GAMES AND TASKS

Color Memory Game
Put several different colored objects in a box.

Discuss the objects and the color of each.

Children take turns picking up an object and without looking recall its color.

Reading Readiness Task
Place different colored and sized objects in a row.

Children describe them from left to right (for example, a small blue triangle, a large orange hexagon, a medium red hexagon).

Shape or Color Boards
String with magnets or pins on the end is attached to each shape or color on the left.

The child matches these to the corresponding shape or color on the right.

If using magnets, affix a nail or paper clip behind each shape or color.

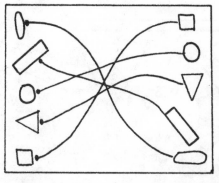

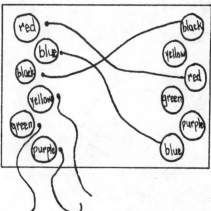

Sorting Tasks
IN A POCKET CHART OR BOXES
The child sorts according to the labels on the pockets or boxes.

These may be colors, shapes, textures, or numbers.

Pictures or actual objects may be used.

ON A PEGBOARD
The teacher places one card on the top hook.

The child chooses appropriate cards to place on the other hooks.

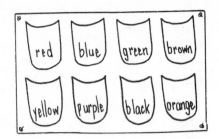

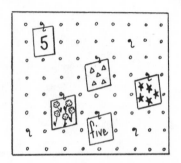

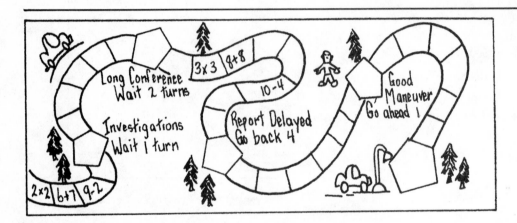

Pentagon
Two to four players participate.

Each player rolls dice and moves the appropriate number of spaces.

If the phonetic or arithmetic question is answered correctly, the child may stay on the square.

If the child is unable to answer, he or she goes back to the beginning.

The first to reach the pentagon is the winner.

Sponges may be easily cut with scissors and numbered with felt pens to make quiet dice for these floor and table games.

Venn Diagrams

Children begin by sorting large objects and attribute blocks or logic blocks.

As progress is made they sort pictures of objects and, eventually, they can sort words.

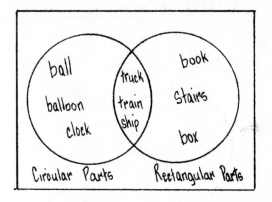

Shape Chase

Two to four players participate.

Each player rolls dice and moves to the next shape named.

The first child to the end of the track is the winner.

Transparent adhesive vinyl offers sturdy protection for your games and oversized workcards or mounted photographs. A narrow rim of vinyl extending over the edges prevents the card from peeling.

Transparencies can be made from glossy magazine pictures with the aid of adhesive vinyl. Simply place the vinyl over the picture; firmly rub the entire surface with the back of a spoon; and then soaking it in water, remove the picture. Voilá! You now have an inexpensive colored transparency.

Domino Shapes

The teacher or the children can make many simple domino games from colored cardboard of various shapes.

The domino pieces are labeled with numbers, number names, shapes, or shape names.

The games are played as regular dominoes with the child matching the numbers or shapes.

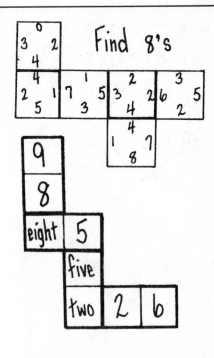

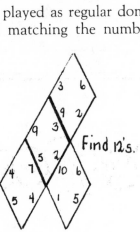

Sequencing Shapes or Colors

Two players participate.

The caller says "circle, triangle, square," or "red, blue, green, black," and so on.

The player must listen carefully and place his or her shape or color cards down in the correct order.

When the player misses, he becomes the caller.

The caller calls two cards, or as many as eight in order to make the game more difficult.

Line-a-Shape

The child cuts out pictures from magazines.

He looks for and outlines the basic shapes.

Pictures are then used for display or they can be used to make a shape collage.

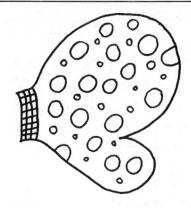

Mystery Mittens

Large mittens may be sewn, knitted, or crocheted so that a child may put in both hands, feel an object and describe its texture, shape, or a combination of size, texture, and shape.

Word Worms

The child prints like words on circles and glues them together to create a word worm.

Children try to see how long a worm they can make.

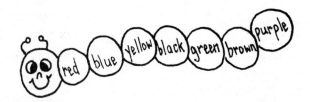

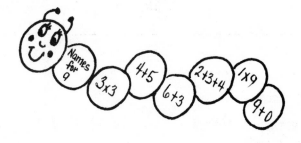

Help Me Color This

The teacher makes a large drawing and the children take turns coloring various sections according to specific instructions (for example, a number code, or a shape code is printed inside the sections).

An example of a number code:

1 = yellow, 2 = blue, 3 = brown, 4 = green, and 5 = red

Mysterious Shapes

Cut different shapes out of sandpaper and mount them on cards.

The child closes his or her eyes, feels the shape, and guesses what it is.

Arithmetic Flags

Each child has a flag with a number printed on it.

The teacher shows an equation and children with the right answer raise their flags.

Flags showing colors or shapes could be used with younger children.

Missing Shape Game

Several shapes are placed on the floor.

One child hides his or her eyes while one or more shapes are removed.

The child must be able to name the missing shape or shapes.

This game may also be played with colors, numbers, patterns, or textures.

Shape-O

Three to seven players participate.

This is played in the same way as bingo.

The caller may say "circle" or show a picture of a circular object.

SHAPE-O			
Row 1	Row 2	Row 3	Row 4
○	△	▱	◐
◐	□	⏢	△
⏢	◐	□	◇
□	▱	△	○

Color-O

This is played in the same manner as the previous game, substituting colors for shapes.

COLOR-O			
Row 1	Row 2	Row 3	Row 4
red	green	blue	brown
blue	yellow	green	red
purple	orange	brown	yellow
yellow	red	orange	purple

PROJECTS

Construction

This is based on triangular, rectangular, and square shapes using any of the following:

balsa wood

straws

boxes of various sizes

wooden blocks

attribute blocks or logic blocks

pretzels and marshmallows

Tinkertoys

The children may be directed to aim for height, balance, strength, size, or to copy a specific building type or object, such as a train.

Collections

Bulletin board or table displays of particular colors, shapes, textures, lines, or patterns may be made.

Objects are collected at home, outdoors, or in school.

Individual children, small groups, or the whole class may be assigned a collection task.

Small patio tables are superb for displaying collections, books, special workcards, or items of interest. Plastic or lightweight metal tables are inexpensive and are invaluable during the summer months at your home or cottage.

Color Days

The teacher calls special color days on which the children work basically with that color—for example, on "Orange Day" the children would:

> wear something orange

> do their work on orange paper

> mix orange paint and use this along with orange crayons, wool, paper, etc., for their handwork

You might even serve cheese, oranges, or carrots for snacks, or give happy face seals made from orange gummed paper for good work.

You can even look at the world through orange-colored glasses! Large masks or glasses are made by taping or stapling colored cellophane to cardboard frames. String ties or elastic headbands allow the children to wear these glasses and receive a different view of their surroundings. Excellent for promoting discussion and story writing.

Finding Shapes and Lines

The children are assigned to look for lines and shapes in nature, the school, the home, and the community (in general, or perhaps in a specific park or building).

If possible, they should collect, sort, and classify items or draw, record, and tally their findings.

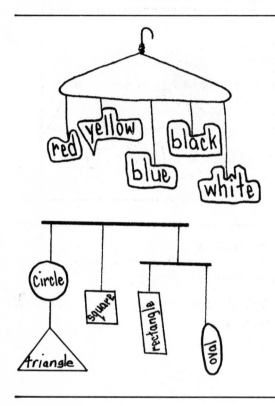

Mobiles

The children construct their own mobiles using:

>   colored paper or objects

>   configurated color, pattern, texture, shape, or line words

>   drawn and cut shapes

>   magazine pictures exhibiting particular shapes, patterns, lines, or colors

>   three-dimensional objects gathered from home or school

HANDWORK

Cut and Paste

Children trace, cut, and paste paper shapes of various sizes and colors to make designs and patterns or specified objects and pictures.

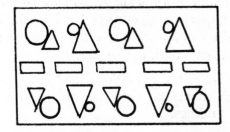

Paper Tearing

Pictures are made by tearing shapes or picture pieces from colored paper.

They are then pasted onto a large paper to complete the picture.

Experimenting with Color

Pictures or designs are painted using:

      one of the primary colors (red, yellow, and blue)

      two of the primary colors

      all three of the primary colors

      two of the primary colors mixed in varying proportions to make secondary colors

Collages

These can be of a specified color and involve materials of varying patterns and textures.

Encourage the children to:

use a wide variety of materials, such as string, ribbon, construction paper, tissue paper, cellophane, crepe paper, straws, pipe cleaners, fabric, magazine pictures, paint

fold, bend, curl, cut, glue, and staple the materials to form interesting combinations and effects

Texture Paintings

These can be made by adding tea leaves, sand, or other insoluble granular substances to prepared paint.

Concentric Shapes

A shape is glued or stapled to the center of the drawing paper.

The child then draws and colors in bands of increasing size around the shape.

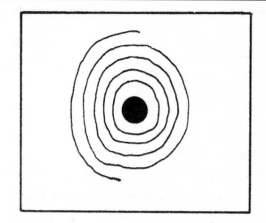

Small fingers may find it easier to handle oversized crayons. Recycle your old crayon bits by melting them down in tin cans and remolding them in pill bottles, tiny paper cups, or egg cartons.

PHYSICAL ACTIVITIES

Movements

Move forward in a small or large circle, square, rectangle, or triangle.

Move backward in a small or large circle, square, rectangle, or triangle.

Hop, run, walk, skip, jump, roll in a circle, square, rectangle, triangle, figure eight, or zigzag pattern.

Use one part of the body as a pivot point and rotate in a circle around it.

Use another part of the body to make a circle, square, rectangle, or triangle.

Make yourself into a cone, sphere, or cylinder.

Make yourself into a sphere and roll.

Run and jump to form a sphere, cone, or cylinder.

Make yourself as small, tall, big, or wide as you can.

Move, using:

> two feet and two hands
>
> two feet and one hand
>
> one foot and two hands
>
> one foot and one hand

Move, taking:

> three large steps and three small steps
>
> one giant step and seven short hops
>
> backward and forward steps

Pyramids

This activity incorporates:

> three, five, seven or more children
>
> benches or heavy wooden chairs
>
> hoops, ropes, or bean bags

These should be done on mats for safety.

Divide the children into groups, and after a few basic safety instructions and a discussion of what a pyramid is, let them devise their own pyramids.

Shape and Line Maze

Arrange a large maze of shapes and lines on the floor using masking or cloth tape.

Give the children instructions which will enable them to move around the maze.

For example, hop around the circle, roll around the square, walk along the two parallel lines, and jump over the small triangle.

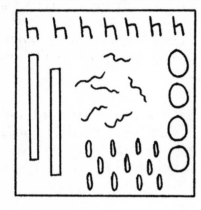

Equipment Maze

Set up a maze using a combination of small equipment (for example, mats, ropes, chairs, skittles, hoops, bean bags, and benches).

Set specific tasks for the children to accomplish with each piece or grouping of equipment.

Explain the entire maze and all the tasks to the children before they begin (try to incorporate as much of the unit vocabulary as you can).

For example, set the equipment in a square pattern.

Give the following instructions:

run twice around the outside of the square

weave a zigzag line through the chairs

jump from the first hoop to the second, then into the third and fourth

move along the parallel benches with two feet and two hands

skip ten times

WORKSHEETS

Page 32

Count and Color The child looks for and counts various shapes, and colors them the appropriate color.

Pages 33, 34, 35, 36, 37

Fill-ins The teacher prints arithmetic equations or phonetically spelled words in the shapes. The teacher may print on the stencil or print individualized questions on each duplicated page. The child completes each equation or word. These pages may also be used to promote creative ideas and drawings, in the same manner as the Line Drawings. See page 14.

Pages 38, 39

Shape Train Scramble The child colors the shapes on page 39 in appropriate colors and cuts them out. He then assembles and pastes them onto a piece of paper to make a train that is the same as the original, or pastes them on top of the corresponding shapes on the original train.

Page 40

Tangram Patterns See WORKCARDS, page 3.

Page 41

Three Things See WORKCARDS, page 7.

Page 42

Cut and Paste The teacher prints arithmetic equations or phonetic words on the shapes of the turtle, and the corresponding answers or phonetic sounds on the shapes to the left. The children must cut out the shapes and paste them on top of the appropriate place.

Page 43

Think and Draw The child draws three things that contain the named shape. The child may print the name of the object he has drawn.

Page 44, 45, 46

Line Drawings These pages may be cut along the double line and stapled, together with lined paper, to make creative writing booklets; or each of the six pages may be given to the pupils separately. The child may turn his or her paper in any position to draw a picture incorporating the teacher-made figure.

Page 47

Sort-a-Word The child sorts words into the shapes. The teacher may tell the pupils that they are sorting for shapes, patterns, and surface texture, or they may be allowed to discover this for themselves.

Page 48

Box Patterns See WORKCARDS, page 13.

If paste is applied only to the top portion of the shape, the answer shapes will flip up so that the worksheet can be corrected.

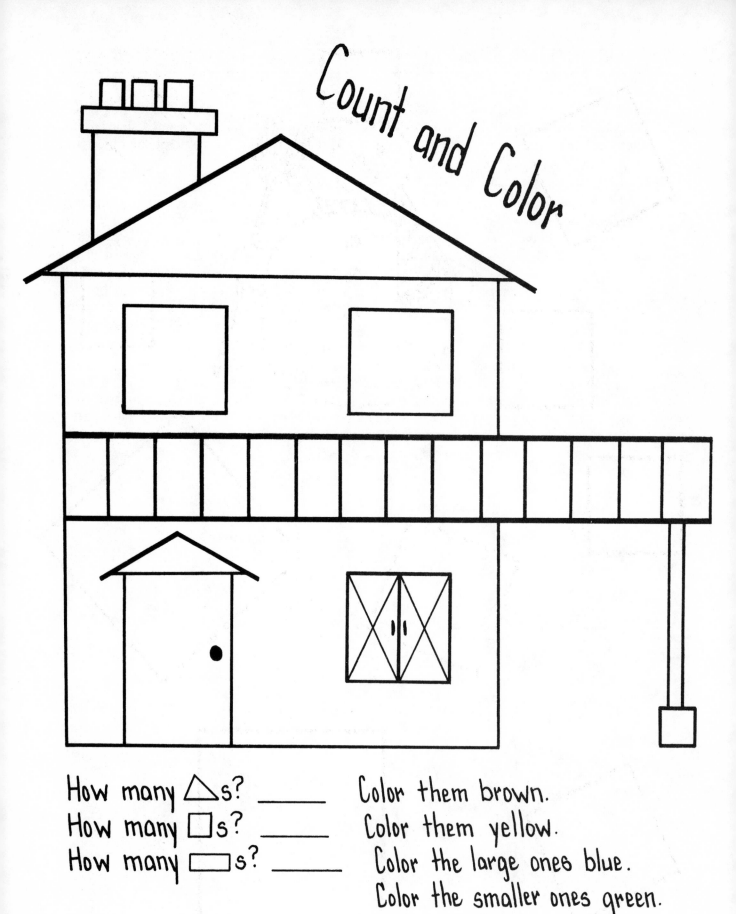

Count and Color

How many △s? _____ Color them brown.

How many □s? _____ Color them yellow.

How many ▭s? _____ Color the large ones blue.

Color the smaller ones green.

JEFF'S MOVING
AND STORAGE

From *Totalaction* © 1980 by Goodyear Publishing Company, Inc.

Three Things

Think and Draw

cylinder			
cone			
sphere			
cube			
pyramid			
prism			

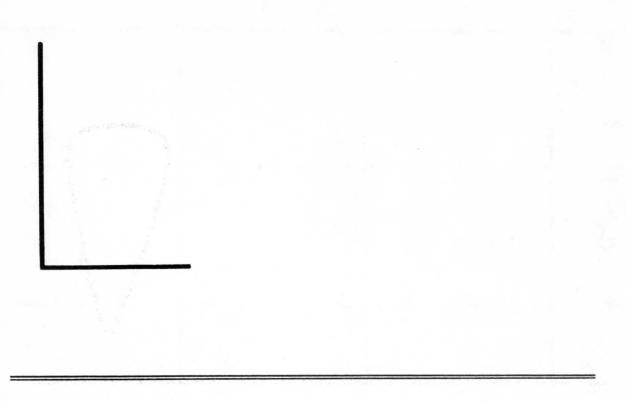

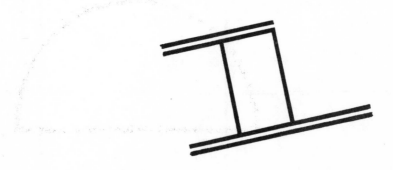

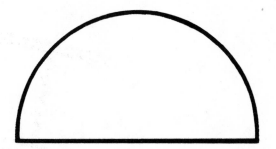

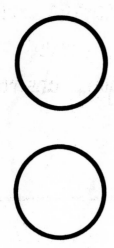

_____

ℓℓℓ

rough, circle, diamond, polka dot, smooth, paisley, shiny, square, trapezoid, stripes, triangle, dull, rectangle, solid, plaid, soft, oval, bumpy, rhombus, tartan, even, pentagon, hard, semicircle, check, uneven, curved, flat, herringbone, hexagon, hound's tooth, octagon, abstract, parallelogram

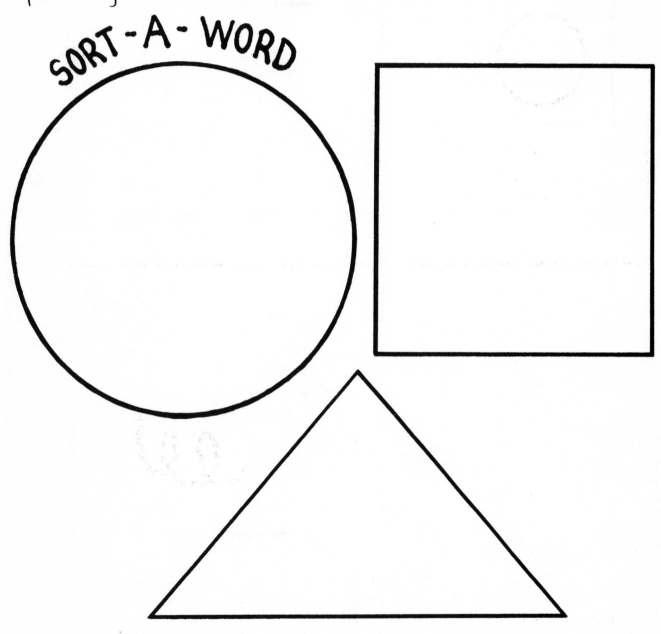

SORT - A - WORD

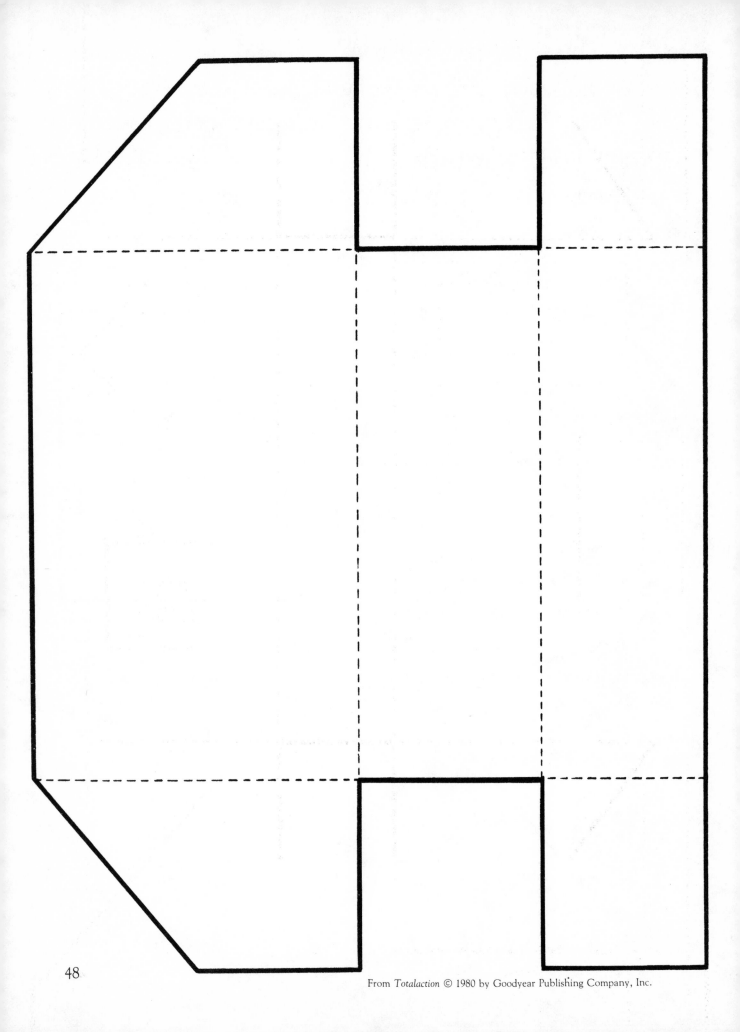

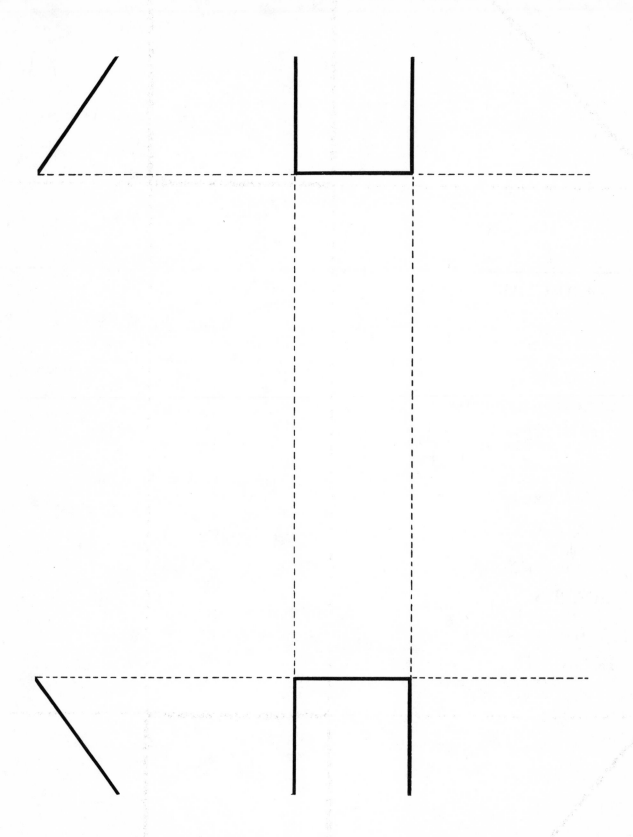

VOCABULARY
Animal Names
Performer Names
Equipment Names
Sensory and Descriptive Words
Skill Words

WORKCARD SETS
What's Missing?
Popcorn Poof! Ideas to Promote
  Creative Speaking and Writing
Make a Set
Feet, Feet, Feet!
If
Big Bonnie
Balancing
Sights and Sounds

GRAPHS
Graphing Ideas
Types of Graphs

BOOKLETS
Child-made Booklets
Class-made Booklets

GAMES AND TASKS
Come to the Circus
Missing Animals or Clowns
Balloon Man
Pin the Nose on the Clown
Tent Toss
Concentration
Greater Than, Less Than, Equal To
Money Makers
Climbing High
Leopold Lion
Elephants Walk in Circus Rings
Sorting Carts
Concession
Cracking the Whip
Sound Cans
Sound Discrimination
Venn Diagrams

PROJECTS
Posters and Advertising
Circus Day
Models, Dioramas, and Construction
Concession Stand
Puppets
Research
Mobiles

CIRCUS SIGHTS AND SOUNDS

HANDWORK
Clown Hats
Plasticene, Clay-Dough or Clay
  Animals
Finger Painting
"C" Animals
Balloon Heads
Configuration Animals
Stand-up Animals
Paper Strip Clown
Be a Clown!
Paper Bag or Box Animals
Beasts

PHYSICAL ACTIVITIES
Hoops
Ropes
Balance Beam or Bench
Trampoline
Tumbling
Rhythm Balls
Movement to Music
Movement Instructions

WORKSHEETS
Fill-ins
Finish Me
Configurations
Who's Balancing This Ball?
Find Sixteen Hidden Letters
Cut and Paste
Big Bonnie
A Set Of

SKILLS

The core and basis of this thematic unit is the development of the following skills:

recognition and understanding of the unit vocabulary

recognition of circus animals, performers, and equipment

awareness of physical abilities and skills

discrimination and classification of sounds, smells, and sizes

interpretation of moods and rhythm in music

awareness of details

investigation using nonstandard units of measure

knowledge, interpretation, and creation of graphs

ability to follow oral and written directions

expansion of verbal and nonverbal creative expression

interpretation and investigation of the denominational value of money

ability to carry out basic research

growth of gross and fine motor skills

reinforcement of phonetic sounds

reinforcement of basic number facts

development of recall skills

VOCABULARY

Animal Names
lion, lioness, tiger, giraffe, elephant, kangaroo, seal, horse, bear, camel, monkey

Performer Names
clown, lion tamer, juggler, tightrope walker, aerialist, cyclist, trainer, bareback rider, ringmaster, acrobat

Equipment Names
net, tightrope, rope, ring, tent, swing, unicycle, bicycle, motorcycle, whip, cage, ladder, torch, stilts, hoops, tub, barrel, cannon, sword

Sensory and Descriptive Words
loud, soft, squeaky, crash, bang, chatter, roar, boom, whinny, cry, laugh, trumpet, bark, growl, noisy, quiet, hush, strong, weak, huge, tiny, small, fat, thin, skinny, enormous, gigantic, gross, beautiful, amusing, funny, applause, cheers, hoorays

Skill Words
dainty, agile, clever, graceful, clumsy, coordinated, balance, juggle, ride, dance, talent, somersault, skip, jump, hop, leap, prance, cartwheel, tumble, forward roll, vault

WORKCARD SETS

What's Missing?
The child looks at the picture and tells or
writes what is missing.

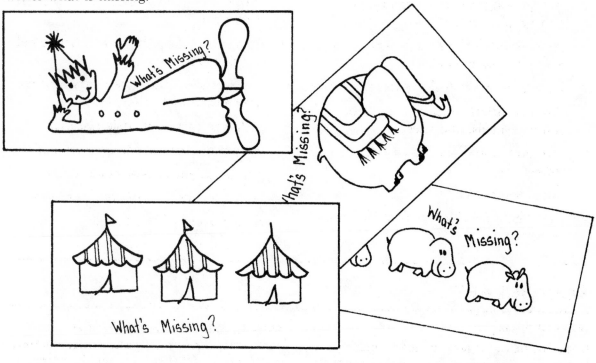

Popcorn Poof! Ideas to Promote Creative Speaking and Writing

After my first kernel, I began to dis-appear _____

Everytime I ate one piece, my bag got larger and _____

I chose my favorite caramel corn, but when I tasted it, it was _____

One night I dreamed I worked in a pop-corn factory and _____

The contest had started! Who would eat the most popcorn _____

A little man gave me a magic popcorn popper and _____

As I went to pay for my popcorn—my money disappeared _____

At first my popcorn tasted good, but then I found _____

As I reached for my first kernel of popcorn, I heard a little voice cry, "Don't eat me!" _____

The butter in my popcorn suddenly started to turn purple _____

For ease of marking and to prevent losses, have the children clip the workcards to the matching worksheet, their papers, notebooks, or booklets when they have completed the assignments.

Designated places for collecting these finished assignments are invaluable. You may denote several cubbyholes, decorated boxes, ice-cream buckets, shelves, file folders, record racks, or fabric sacks for this purpose. There should be separate places for each group, subject, or type of activity; thus facilitating the locating and marking of student work. You may even denote large cartons or plastic tubs for collecting completed handwork assignments.

Make a Set
Make a set of:

 things that are strong

 things that you can cuddle

 tall things

 things that make you laugh

 fat things

 things that can hop

 things you can ride

 things that make noise

 big things

 things with big feet

 things with big noses

 people in the circus

 animals in the circus

The child chooses or is given a card and prints or draws the appropriate set members in a notebook or on a corresponding mimeo (see WORKSHEETS, page 91).

Feet, Feet, Feet!
The teacher makes several clown feet from colored cardboard.

The child chooses a workcard and uses the feet to carry out the assignment.

A record of the child's findings are kept on paper feet or in a foot-shaped notebook.

Measure:

 the classroom

 your desk

 your notebook

 the chalkboard

 the distance to the principal's office

 the distance to the nearest exit

 the width of the window

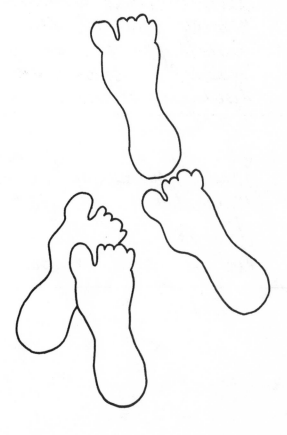

the piano
the distance to the gym
a pile of blocks
your painting
your friend
a big animal
a small animal

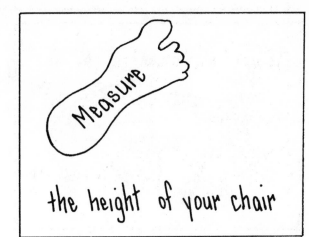

the height of your chair

So, you've cut out all those feet for measuring. Why not lend them another function? They can arouse interest and introduce your measuring work. Here's what you do. Attach the feet in various places around the classroom. They may walk in the door, climb in a window, suddenly appear on the ceiling, or leave a path to follow. Who or what made the footprints? What do they look like? Why did they come? How did they get here? Where have they gone? Will they come back? You can encourage the children to explore such questions through drawings, discussion, stories, poetry, and drama.

You can give the character or footprints certain traits, or perhaps find a secret message of explanation.

You can use handprints, eyes, or bright spots in the same manner.

If

These workcards can be used to encourage oral or written expression, and require the children to transform their words into pictures.

For variation, one child might be asked to make taped interviews of oral responses to a specific question.

If you lived in the circus, what would you do?

If I gave you six balls, what would you do?

If I gave you a lion, what would you do?

If I gave you a unicycle, what would you do?

If I gave you four hoops, what would you do?

If you had twenty-three balloons, what would you do?

If you had huge feet, what would you do?

If you were the ringmaster, what would you do?

If you were a trick dog, what would you do?

If no one applauded, what would you do?

If your pet was an elephant, what would you do?

If the tiger escaped from his cage, what would you do?

If the monkey ran away, what would you do?

Big Bonnie

Big Bonnie says, "Make:

eight circus seals."

three dancing bears."

five candy apples."

four elephants holding tails."

two clumsy clowns."

one graceful bareback rider."

three agile cyclists."

one enormous lady."

two growling lions."

one concession stand."

seven tall giraffes."

five big bass drums."

nine waving flags."

These cards may include all of the unit vocabulary according to the ability of the children.

A corresponding mimeo could be made (see WORKSHEETS, page 90) for the child to print and illustrate each statement on his or her workcard.

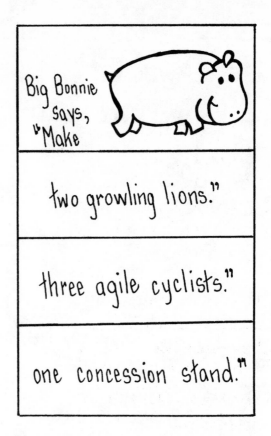

Big Bonnie says, "Make

two growling lions."

three agile cyclists."

one concession stand."

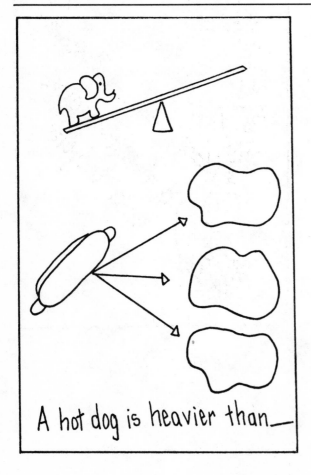

A hot dog is heavier than___

Balancing

Unlike other sets of workcards which require the children to actually balance objects, this set calls for the children to make interpretive judgments.

Three answers are printed or drawn for each workcard.

An elephant is lighter than _____.

A unicycle is lighter than _____.

A hot dog is heavier than _____.

Five chocolate bars are lighter than _____.

A motorcycle is heavier than _____.

A horse is heavier than _____.

Three peanuts are lighter than _____.

A bass drum is heavier than _____.

A clown's shoe is heavier than _____.

Cotton candy is lighter than _____.

Twenty-five peanuts are heavier than _____.

A dog weighs about the same as _____.

A camel weighs about the same as _____.

A scooter weighs about the same as a _____.

A clown's umbrella weighs about the same as _____.

An acrobat weighs about the same as _____.

A bag of popcorn weighs about the same as _____.

_____ weighs about the same as the fat lady.

Sights and Sounds

This set of interpretive workcards builds on the child's knowledge of unit vocabulary and draws upon his or her experiences.

The child chooses a workcard and reads, prints, and illustrates the phrase in a notebook or on a chart.

The phrases may include:

a happy clown and a sad clown

a trainer with four dogs

clowns make children laugh

a juggler with six balls

this goes up and down

this makes lots of noise

this looks delicious

this goes boom, boom, boom

this is fat and funny

this weighs 867 kilograms

three animals doing tricks

a monkey riding on a bicycle

a dancing elephant

a circus parade

a tightrope walker

I would like a ride on this train

Sights and Sounds

to read, print and illustrate—
a monkey riding on a bicycle

The toy departments in many stores carry small, very inexpensive rubber stamp sets. They usually contain stamps of letters, numbers, and often interesting characters or animals. These stamps, along with ink pads in two or three colors, will serve many purposes. Keep them ready for stamping good work, completing charts, and decorating workcards or booklets.

Children love to use the letters in printing phonics lists, spelling words or special messages, and the numbers in making arithmetic equations or patterns.

It's fun to make your own stamps, too — draw a simple design on an eraser and carve away the unwanted portions. You can make handy stamps of your initials and of unit symbols or characters.

GRAPHS

Graphing Ideas

my favorite performer

color of clowns' hair

most difficult act

things sold in the concession stand

number of animals in the circus

what I ate at the circus

children in our class who went to the circus

different kinds of cycles

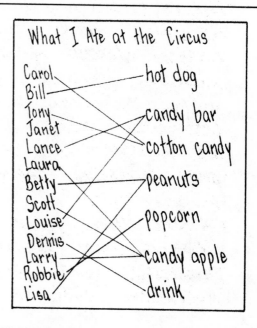

What I Ate at the Circus

Carol
Bill
Tony
Janet
Lance
Laura
Betty
Scott
Louise
Dennis
Larry
Robbie
Lisa

hot dog
candy bar
cotton candy
peanuts
popcorn
candy apple
drink

My Favorite Performer

lion tamer ■ ■ ■ ■

clown ■ ■ ■ ■ ■ ■ ■

acrobat ■ ■ ■ ■ ■

juggler ■ ■ ■

bareback rider ■

aerialist ■ ■ ■ ■

cyclist ■ ■ ■

tightrope walker ■ ■

Types of Graphs

picture

bar

line

matching

set graphs

BOOKLETS

Child-made Booklets
wild animal booklets

circus performer booklets

sights at the circus

sounds at the circus

fun at the circus

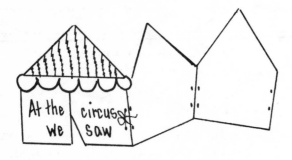

Class-made Booklets
my favorite circus act

what we saw at the circus

clowns

GAMES AND TASKS

Come to the Circus
Two to four players participate.

Each player rolls dice and moves the appropriate number of spaces.

If the phonetic or arithmetic question is answered correctly, the child may stay on the space.

If the child is unable to answer, he goes back to the beginning.

The first to reach the circus tent is the winner.

Missing Animals or Clowns
A hoop is placed on the floor.

Various toy animals or clowns are placed inside the hoop.

One child covers his or her eyes while one or more animals or clowns are removed.

The child has to guess what is missing.

Balloon Man

Words, phrases, or equations are printed on the balloons.

If a child can read or answer the balloons he may:

> stick his name card in the man's hat band
>
> stick his own tie on the man
>
> have a balloon to create something with at the handwork center

Pin the Nose on the Clown

Two to four players participate.

This is played in the same way as pin-the-tail-on-the-donkey.

Tent Toss

Two to four players participate.

Players take turns tossing rings over wooden or cardboard cone-shaped tents.

Each player has three tosses, and must total his or her score after each turn.

The teacher may set a time limit, and the winner is the player with the highest score.

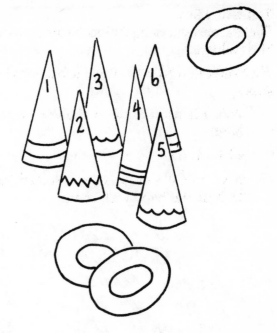

For these open-ended games, make sure that you and the children set your own well-defined time limits. In this way you can avoid squabbles. In circle games, perhaps the last child to play will start the game next time. Some suggestions for setting time limits are: play may continue for five minutes, until six children have played, until all the cards have been turned over, for five turns each, until cleanup time, or until the timer runs out.

Concentration

The teacher makes matching pairs of circus cards using decorative gummed seals, cut-out pictures, or hand-drawn pictures.

Pictures are placed face down.

The two players take turns trying to find matching pairs; if they do, they keep the pair.

The winner is the player with the most pairs of cards.

A host of decorative gummed seals are available in card shops, stationery departments, and teacher stores. They range from simple shapes to seals of cartoon characters, interesting themes, and special occasions. And in your classroom they can serve a variety of uses: rewarding good work; creating story starters; making cards for matching, sorting, and concentration games; decorating labels and game boards; enhancing, and perhaps even giving ideas for workcards; and creating shape patterns for the children to copy.

Greater Than, Less Than, Equal To

The teacher makes various cards.

The children spread these cards on the floor, count the objects on each and match as many cards as they can.

If there are two players, one keeps time and checks for correctness, while the other matches as quickly as possible.

For variation, pieces of magnetic tape could be glued to the backs of the cards.

Money Makers

Two players participate.

One child chooses a money card and places it face up in the middle of the board.

The other player must quickly choose coins from the money bag and place them appropriately on the spaces. For example:

50¢ = 5 dimes
    = 2 quarters
    = 50 pennies
    = 4 dimes, 1 nickel, 5 pennies

Climbing High

The teacher draws a tightrope and a ladder.

Each child makes a paper acrobat and puts his or her name on it.

Sight words or arithmetic equations are placed on the rungs of the ladder.

Children try to climb to the tightrope by reading the words or answering the equations on the ladder.

If a child misses a word or an equation, his or her acrobat sits on that rung.

Leopold Lion

The teacher makes a lion face and cuts a large opening for the mouth, behind which a paper bag is pasted.

The teacher makes cards with phonetic words, circus words, or arithmetic equations.

Leopold Lion is only able to eat cards following the teacher's instructions.

The children must read or answer cards correctly in order to feed Leopold.

Elephants Walk in Circus Rings

Two to four players, each with two markers, participate.

Taking turns, each child rolls both a vowel and a number die.

A player moves his or her place marker from elephant to elephant according to the number die and must make a word beginning with the consonant on the elephant and using the vowel he has rolled.

If a player is unable to make a word, he stays on the same elephant and tries again on his next turn.

As a player passes the flags he moves his ring marker to the next flag.

The winner is the first player to land on flag number four.

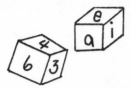

Sorting Carts

Circus carts are made out of cereal or shoe boxes.

Children collect and/or sort objects according to the teacher's directions.

Instructions can be printed directly on each cart or changeable instruction cards could be clipped to the sides.

Concession

Two to four players participate.

Each counts out one dollar in change and places marker on space with arrow.

Players move according to roll of dice, buying articles from the "concession stand" and placing matching cards on the spaces.

After all the articles are bought, any player landing on another player's possession must pay the owner the indicated tax.

Each time a player lands on a money space, he rolls the dice and collects the money indicated by the roll; for example, if a player rolls six, he would collect six cents.

The winner is the player with the most money.

The teacher sets the playing time limit.

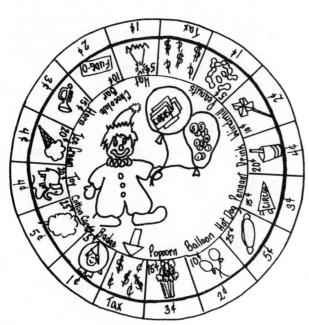

Cracking the Whip

The children stand in a ring and the teacher chooses one child to be "it."

"It" stands in the middle of the ring pretending to be a circus master cracking his or her whip.

He says, "I am tired of cracking my whip." The other children all ask, "Why?" "It" says, "Because the elephants won't walk in the ring swinging their trunks."

"It" may suggest any activity he wants and the other children act out the instructions.

"It" chooses a new circus master from the ring of performers and the game continues.

Sound Cans

Decorated coffee cans, paint cans, nut cans, or any cans with reusable lids may be used.

The teacher places objects inside and seals the cans.

The children shake the cans and listen carefully in order to identify the contents, or to match the cans with similar sounds.

Sound Discrimination

Records or tape recordings can be used to help the children recognize and differentiate animal and circus sounds.

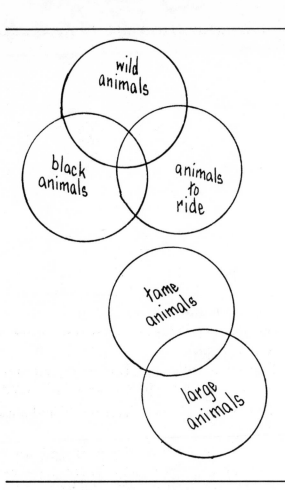

Venn Diagrams

The teacher introduces various types of Venn diagrams depending on the ability of the children.

The children may sort actual objects, pictures, or words.

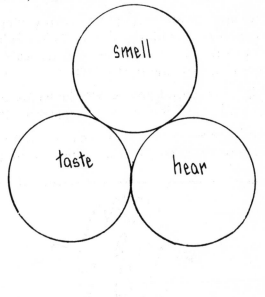

PROJECTS

Posters and Advertising

Groups or individuals make large posters for advertising.

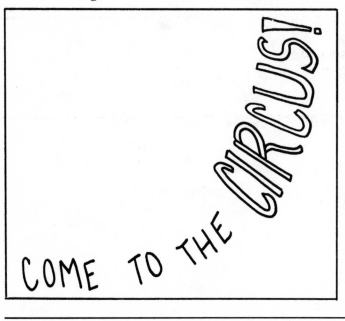

Circus Day

The posters from the previous project may be used to advertise a class circus or circus day.

The children may dress up and perform "acts" including the movement education activities taught in this unit.

Pets may be brought to take part.

Parents or other classes may be invited for the performance.

Admission may be charged and donated to a school fund or to a local charity.

Models, Dioramas, and Construction
Some ideas are:

> tents which may be small models or child sized
>
> models showing various circus acts
>
> animals from clay, blocks, pipe cleaners, wires
>
> circus train from shoe or cereal boxes, or from large cardboard boxes which children can actually get into
>
> circus puppet theater
>
> concession stand

Printing stories, captions, and identifications for handwork, projects, paintings, and displays is much faster when you have a supply of precut labels. Lightweight cardboard is best for labels since it will stand alone if folded back near the bottom edge. A variety of sizes from small (3" x 5", 8 cm x 13 cm) to large (9" x 12", 23 cm x 30 cm) is very convenient.

Concession Stand

A concession stand may be constructed from large cardboard boxes, wood, or corrugated cardboard.

Children may work in groups to decorate and set up the stand.

Popcorn, lollipops, or candy apples can be made in class and sold in the stand for real or play money.

RECIPE FOR TOFFEE APPLES

12 small apples—washed and dried
2 lb (1 kg) caramels
4 tbsp (56 ml) water

Place caramels and water in top of double boiler and heat, stirring until they melt into a smooth mixture.

Dip skewered apples into the sauce, twirling them until they are completely coated.

Set apples upside down on a piece of foil to dry.

If refrigerated, apples will harden in a few minutes.

RECIPE FOR CIRCUS POPS

2 cups (454 ml) white sugar
½ cup (114 ml) light corn syrup
sticks (bamboo skewers)
¼ cup (57 ml) water
food coloring
yields 24 small pops

Mix sugar, corn syrup, and water in a small, heavy pot.

Place over medium heat and stir with a wooden spoon until the mixture begins to boil.

Heat, without disturbing until a candy thermometer reads 310°F (154°C).

If you don't have a thermometer, spoon out a small amount of the syrup and drop it into cold water; if the ball that forms is hard and brittle, the candy is ready.

Remove from heat and stir in food coloring.

Immediately spoon out the mixture onto the shiny side of a length of aluminum foil.

Working quickly before the candy hardens, place a stick or skewer into each pop.

Let cool for a half-hour before removing from foil.

RECIPE FOR CARAMEL CORN

1½ tbsp (21 ml) melted butter
6 tbsp (84 ml) water
1½ cups (341 ml) brown sugar

Stir all ingredients until sugar is dissolved.

Bring to a boil; cover and cook for about three minutes; uncover and cook, without stirring, to the soft ball stage.

Pour mixture over about 6 cups (1.4 l) of popcorn and gently stir with a wooden spoon until well coated.

Spread on shiny side of tin foil to cool.

Puppets

HAND PUPPETS

The children use their imaginations to make puppets from:

- socks
- paper bags
- small boxes
- fabric
- bleach bottles
- light bulbs covered with papier-mâché
- balloons covered with papier-mâché
- mittens

FINGER PUPPETS

Circus figures can be drawn and cut from paper or light cardboard.

The child's fingers become various parts of the puppet's body.

STICK PUPPETS

Paper figures are attached to stick handles.

MARIONETTES

The children can create puppets with movable body parts using a combination of paper and paper fasteners, or fabric and strings.

Research

Children may work alone or in small groups to research facts on wild or circus animals.

Children are instructed to read books and view films carefully, keeping in mind that what they draw or write about should answer *what, when, where, why, how.*

To prevent direct copying from a book, the children are told to close the books before they begin writing.

Mobiles

Children construct their own mobiles using cut-out pictures, hand-drawn pictures, configurational words, toy animals, or wire or pipe cleaner animals.

With very young children, the mobiles may be made out of coat hangers.

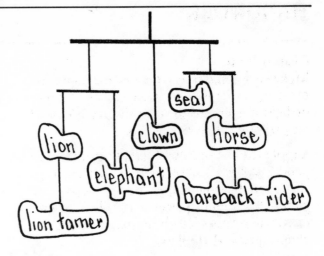

Where are you going to hang all this handwork, and when will you find the time? It's no problem if, at the beginning of the school year, you "wire" your classroom. Stretch several lengths of stovepipe wire across the room; they should be above six feet (1.83 meters), but within easy reach. Fasten the wire to the walls with screw-in eyelets. Then as the handwork is finished, it can easily be hung for display by you or the children. A length of wire running in front of windows is terrific for showing off those transparent creations.

Wire can also serve for hanging curtains, draping paper roofs or banners, drying paintings, displaying double-sided pictures, and posting charts or pictures for group lessons. Articles may be attached to the wire with thread, yarn, pins, staples, paper clips, rings, curtain hooks, tape, clothespins, or — for interesting effects — fishing line or invisible thread. Likewise, hoops, umbrellas, lingerie dryers, and coat hangers can provide interesting means for displaying your pupils' stories, worksheets, drawings, handwork, and projects.

HANDWORK

Clown Hats

Make each child a fitted cone-shaped hat by molding a rectangular piece of heavy paper or light cardboard around the child's head and stapling it so that it fits.

Supply the children with crepe paper, tissue paper, colored construction paper, pipe cleaners, baking cups, paper cups and plates, Styrofoam pieces and balls, egg cartons, paper tubes, cloth remnants, as well as glue, tape, and staplers.

Each child, using any of the materials, is to create his or her own clown hat.

A contest may be held to judge the funniest or most original hat.

These hats may be worn on "Circus Day."

Plasticene, Clay-Dough, or Clay Animals

Children may model animals from plasticene, clay-dough, or clay depending upon the ability of the children and the results desired.

For easy cleanup have the children carry out their plasticene or clay modeling on sheets of waxed paper, sample floor tiles, or small boards covered with adhesive vinyl.

RECIPE FOR CLAY-DOUGH

Mix 1 cup (227 ml) of flour and ½ cup (114 ml) of salt together in a bowl.

Slowly add water until the mixture resembles bread dough, squeezing the dough with your hands until it is smooth.

Store the clay-dough in a plastic bag or container with a lid.

Modeling is done on tin foil.

When the model is finished, bake it on its tin foil at 225°F (105°C).

Small, thin models are baked about 15 minutes on each side; while larger, thick objects can be baked up to one hour on each side.

The model may be colored by adding food coloring to the raw dough or by painting the model after baking.

Clear shellac may be used to protect the finish of the model after baking.

Finger Painting

Children may enjoy finger painting to recorded circus music or to the music used for their movement education.

Encourage the children to express the music through their hands.

If you are using powdered finger paint, shake the paint onto the paper and then add the water with a spray bottle. This makes for easier mixing.

"C" Animals

Circus animals are drawn, colored, or painted using the letter "C" as a base.

Balloon Heads

Animal or clown heads can be made by gluing colored paper features to inflated balloons.

Differences in the size, color, and shape of the balloons add to the variety and uniqueness of the animals or clowns.

Configuration Animals

On a folded piece of construction paper, the child prints the name of his or her favorite circus animal making sure that the tall letters touch the fold.

An outline is drawn around the letters.

The configuration is then cut out and decorated to resemble a realistic or imaginary animal.

Stand-up Animals

Using folded 8" x 8" (20 cm x 20 cm) colored construction paper as a basic body form, many animals may be made.

Beginning opposite the fold, cut out a semicircle while leaving one to two inches on either side; this forms the body with four legs.

A head can be made by adding cut paper features to a basic shape (for example, square, triangle, circle, rectangle).

The head and tail are attached to the body by making a small cut at the base of the neck and the tail and sliding them onto the body.

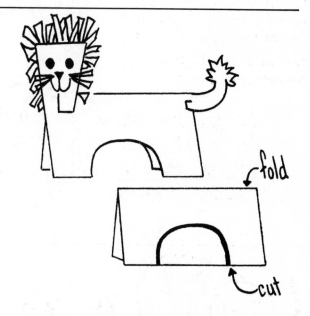

Paper Strip Clown

Paper strips of varying widths and lengths are used to make a clown.

The teacher may have the strips precut for the children's use, or each child may cut his or her own.

Be a Clown!

Life-sized clowns are made by having the children trace each other on large sheets of craft paper or cardboard, adding details such as hats, shoes, clothing, fat tummies, funny faces, hair styles, and balloons as they desire.

The finished drawings are painted, cut out, and may decorate classroom walls or hallways.

Mix powdered paint with liquid soap rather than water for thick paint and denser, more vibrant colors.

Paper Bag or Box Animals

Provide the children with paper lunch bags, boxes of assorted sizes, paper tubes, and egg cartons.

When the children have created the desired body shape, the animal is covered with papier-mâché

When dry, the animal is painted and additional features are added from colored construction paper.

Beasts

Large animals, real or imaginary, can be made from old sheeting or unbleached cotton.

On doubled fabric, trace a child lying on his or her side; add details after the basic shape is traced.

Each piece of fabric is then either tie dyed or painted (or if a printed piece of fabric is used, it may be left as is).

Children may work in groups to make the animals and then take turns sewing the fabric pieces together by hand.

Be sure to leave a large opening for ease in stuffing, or in the case of a very large animal, leave two or three openings.

The animal is then stuffed with shredded newsprint, and the openings are sewn together.

PHYSICAL ACTIVITIES

The following activities may be used in stations, in a teacher-led whole class program, or in a combination of approaches.

Hoops

Roll the hoop with one hand, while running beside it.

Spin the hoop on the floor and run around it until it drops.

Skip with the hoop (frontward, backward).

With the hoop on the floor, jump in and out (frontward, backward, sideways).

Leap or hop over the hoop.

Rotate the hoop on one arm, on the waist, on one foot, on the neck.

Roll the hoop and run through it as it rolls.

Toss the hoop in the air and catch it.

Work the hoop in combination with available music.

Ropes

Fold a skipping rope in half, and swinging it in a circle beside you, jump over it.

Skip frontward and backward, with feet together or alternating feet.

Skip with a partner facing you.

In groups, with two people turning the rope, run through, or run in, skip, and run out.

Skip on the spot slowly, quickly, and very quickly.

Skip, moving around the floor.

Stretch the rope out on the floor, then walk along it, jump over it with two feet (backward, frontward, sideways), and hop over it with one foot (backward, frontward, sideways).

Balance Beam or Bench

Crawl along the beam.

On the stomach, pull self along the beam.

On the back, push self along the beam.

Walk forward and backward, arms held out.

Walk forward and backward on tiptoe.

Walk forward and backward, turning in the middle of the beam.

Walk forward and backward, balancing an object on the head.

Walk sideways on the beam.

Walk forward and step over a bar held above the beam.

Walk forward and pass under a bar held above the beam.

Walk forward and backward, kneel on one knee, then rise and walk to the end of the beam.

Hop on one foot the length of the beam.

Balance on the beam with eyes closed.

Walk forward, backward, and sideways with eyes closed.

Move along the beam imitating the circus animals.

Trampoline

Bounce on the knees, all fours, and the seat.

Bounce on the feet, with a knee drop.

Bounce on the feet, with a seat drop.

Bounce on the feet, making quarter, half, and full turns in the air.

Bounce on the feet, with a back drop.

Bounce with a partner, both synchronously and alternately.

Tumbling

Do log, tuck, forward and backward rolls.

Run, leap, and roll using one or two feet for the takeoff and a log, tuck, forward or backward roll after the landing.

Do a series of rolls.

Link two or three types of rolls together.

Use a springboard trampoline, bench, springboard, or box for variations in leaping.

Rhythm Balls

combinations of tossing, bouncing, and catching

stretching and tossing exercises

stretching and bouncing exercises

tossing and catching using more than one ball

tossing and bouncing to music

combinations of synchronized tossing, bouncing, and catching with a partner

synchronized exercises involving a group or a class (these exercises could be used in creative dance)

Movement to Music

marching   skipping

high stepping   hopping

galloping   running

walking on toes and/or heels

gliding   creeping

turning and   shaking
spinning

leaping   stopping or freezing

Movement Instructions
Move like:

a monkey   a snake

a lion   a clown

a giraffe   a horse

an elephant

Pantomime may evolve.

WORKSHEETS

Page 83
Fill-ins Incomplete arithmetic equations or phonetically spelled words may be printed in the polka dots. The child completes the questions according to the teacher's instructions which are printed in the clown's balloon.

Page 84
Arithmetic or Phonetic Fill-in Incomplete arithmetic equations or words may be printed in the balloons.

Page 85
Finish Me The child completes the clown with pencil and crayons. A story may be written about the finished picture.

Page 86
Configurations The child traces configurations with a pencil or crayon.

Page 87
Who's Balancing This Ball? The child completes the picture showing who is balancing the ball. A story may be written about the finished picture.

Page 88
Find Sixteen Hidden Letters The child finds and lists the hidden letters (i, v, a, n, d, l, m, w, u, j, o, o, e, e, p, c) and scrambles them to make words. Some possibilities are a, an, am, and, wand, dam, jam, pan, can, van, man, land, came, lame, plane, mane, name, cane, vane, lane, woman, in, win, wine, pin, pine, mine, pie, vine, dine, dive, line, lime, dime, on, one, nod, pod, no, low, do, doe, mow, moon, wood, loop, mood, cow, owl, down, clown, mole, pole, vain, jail, pail, mail, join, coin, lion, towel, love, move, dove, poem, come, plum, plume, mule, duel, dual, jewel, view, dew, jump, lump, dump, deep, den, pen, men, women, mend, lend, and new.

Page 89
Cut and Paste Incomplete arithmetic equations are printed on the seals, the answers on the balls. The child cuts along the double line, then cuts out individual balls and pastes each ball so that it balances on the appropriate seal's nose.

Page 90
Big Bonnie See page 57.

Page 91
Make a Set See page 55.

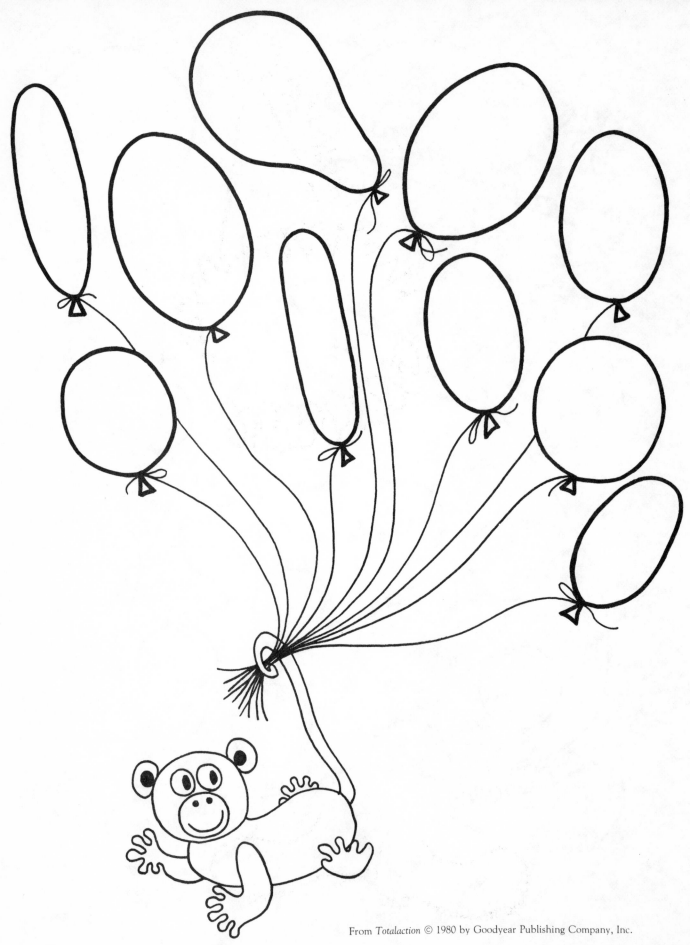

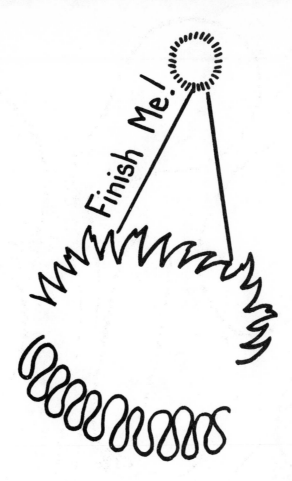

Finish Me!

Configurations

Who's balancing this ball?

Find 16 hidden letters.

List the letters.

_____

_____

Scramble them to make words.

From *Totalaction* © 1980 by Goodyear Publishing Company, Inc.

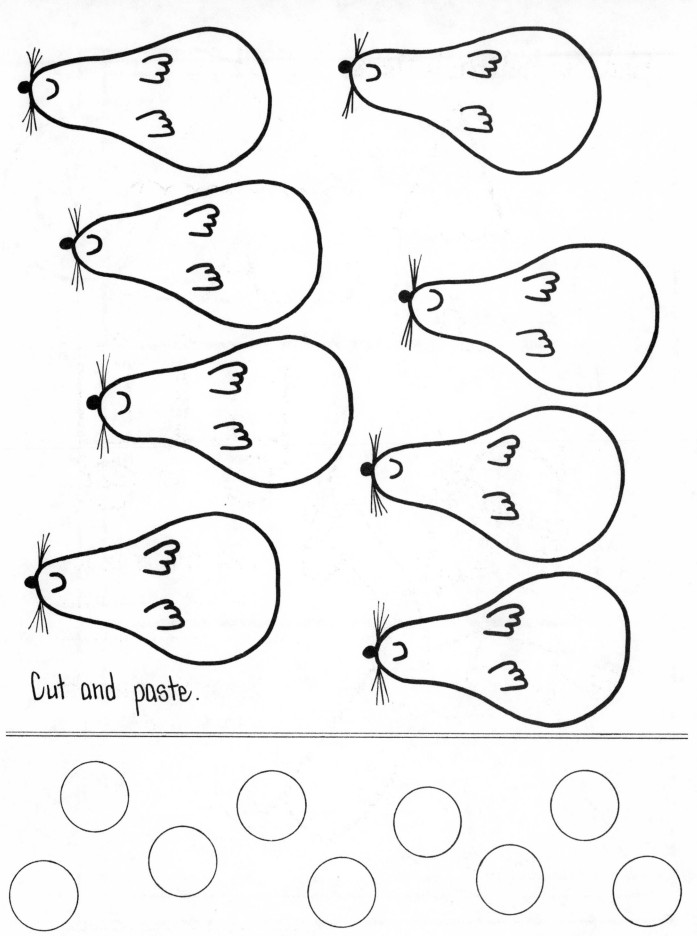

Cut and paste.

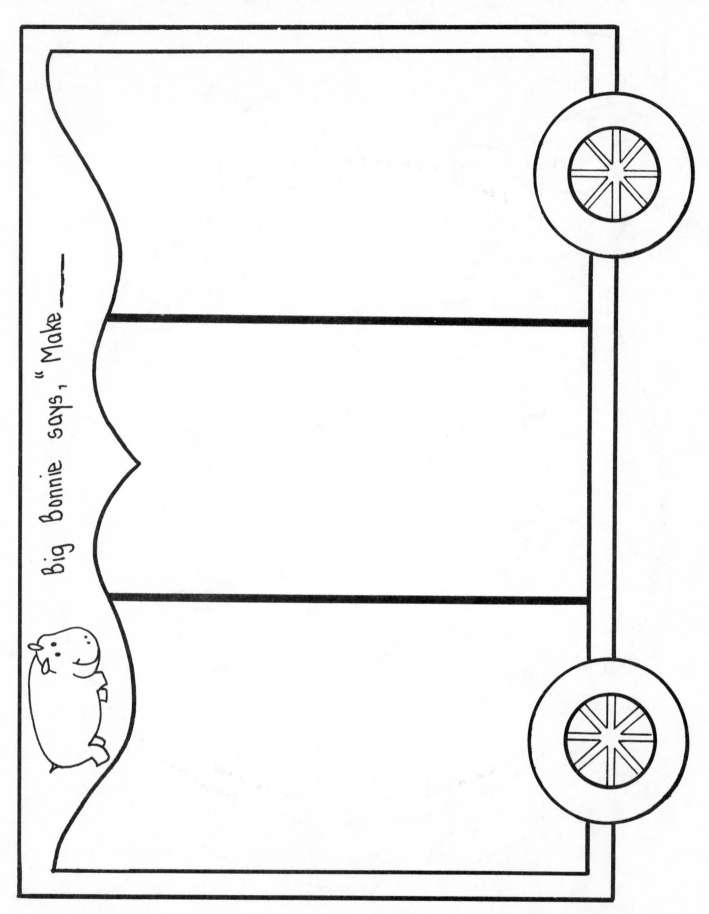

Big Bonnie says, "Make ____

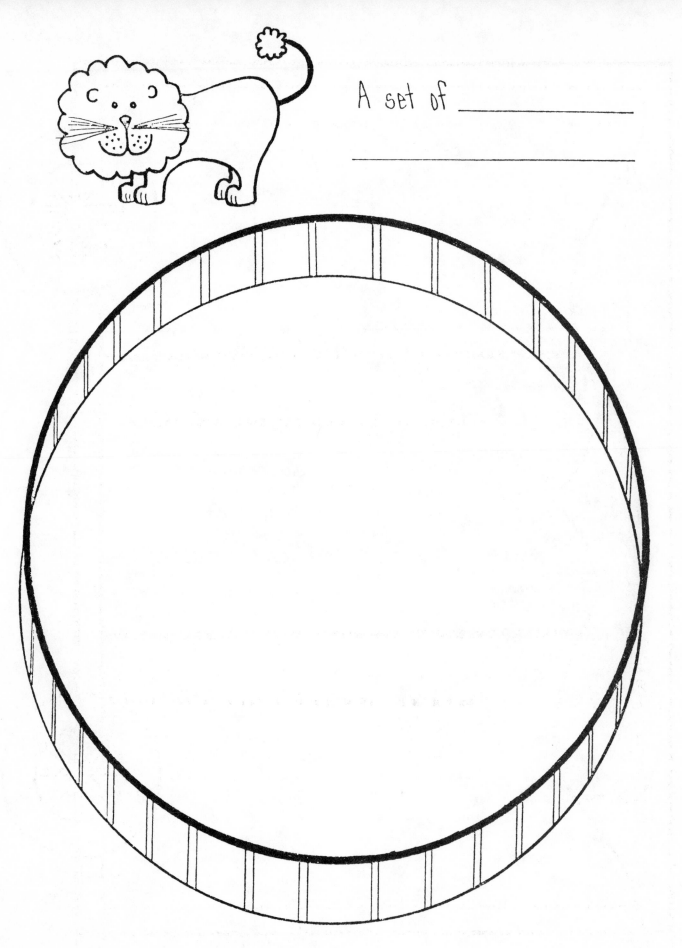

A set of _____

_____

VOCABULARY
Bodies of Water
Land Affected by Water
Water in Motion
Boats
Navigation Terms
Common Parts of a Boat
Fish
Water Animals
Water Life
Man-made Structures Associated With
  Water

BOOKLETS
Child-made Booklets
Class-made Booklets

WORKCARD SETS
Nautical Notes
Anchors Aweigh
If
Parts of the Whole
Story Starters
Thought Waves
Sounders
Versus
Sea Scramble

GAMES AND TASKS
Matching Tasks
Ordering Tasks
Directional Tasks
Floating Pictures
Fishing Fun
Ships' Logs
Water in Motion
List-a-Fish
Fish Bowl
Ship Ahoy!
Water Works
Compound Words
Treasure Hunt
Row, Row, Row Your Boat

WATER, WATER, EVERYWHERE

PROJECTS
Things That Dissolve and Change in Water
Float or Sink
Bridge Construction
Aquariums
Research
Driftwood
Things You Can Do With Sea Shells
Photographic Analysis

HANDWORK
Wax and Tissue
Paper Plate Aquariums
Paper Strip Creatures
Fish
Boats
Clay or Clay-Dough Sea Creatures
Stick or Balsa Rafts
Hole Punch Fish
Plasticene Wash Pictures
Wax Resists

PHYSICAL ACTIVITIES
Bridges
Water Orientation

WORKSHEETS
Fill-ins
Sailing, Sailing
Boats
What Am I?
Above, Below
Sea Shells
The Fisherman
Fish
Dot-to-Dot
Anchors Aweigh
Maze
Crossword Puzzle

SKILLS

The core and basis of this unit is the development of the following skills:

recognition and understanding of the unit vocabulary

differentiation of the bodies of water

investigation of weight and volume measures

expansion of verbal and nonverbal creative expression

knowledge of the types and parts of boats

recognition, classification and investigation of water life

identification of water-related structures and their uses

development of observation skills

differentiation and ordering with respect to size and ordinal position

ability to follow oral and written directions

comprehension of the movements, effects, and uses of water

familiarization with nautical terms

investigation of flotation

construction and examination of bridges

growth of fine motor skills

orientation to the water

reinforcement of phonetic sounds

comprehension and use of compound words

comprehension and use of descriptive words

reinforcement of place value understanding

VOCABULARY

Bodies of Water
ocean, sea, river, lake, stream, pond, brook, bay, inlet, gulf, cove, lagoon, pool, swamp, reservoir, ditch, marsh, bog, slough, spring, waterfall, fiord, harbor

Land Affected by Water
island, peninsula, isthmus, beach, continent, mainland, delta, promontory, highland, lowland, coast, shore, strand, bank, reef, dike, dam, canyon, gorge, ravine

Water in Motion
squirt, splash, spout, rush, gush, sluice, course, ebb, flow, current, tide, race, spring, undercurrent, undertow, eddy, whirlpool, billow, surge, swell, ripple, surf, breakers, tidal wave, run, meander, drip, swirl, dribble, murmur, babble, gurgle, spurt, ooze, choppy, rolling

Boats
barge, canoe, catamaran, dinghy, ferry, freighter, houseboat, Hovercraft, kayak, liner, motorboat, outrigger, raft, rowboat, sailboat, scull, ship, yacht, tanker, trawler, tug, schooner, sloop, ketch, launch, hydroplane, hydrofoil, gondola, cutter, galleon, junk

Navigation Terms
ahead, astern, port, starboard, abeam, amidships, windward, leeward, heave to

Common Parts of a Boat
cabin, bulkhead, berth, deck, companionway, head, galley, helm, keel, porthole, bilge, rudder, running lights, hull, rigging, sail, mast, bow, stern, gunwale, winch, beam, inboard motor, outboard motor, anchor, propeller, turbine, oar, gangplank

Fish
bass, carp, catfish, cod, eel, flounder, halibut, herring, bluefish, mackerel, muskie, perch, pickerel, pipefish, pike, salmon, sardine, smelt, trout, tuna, swordfish, shark, marlin, sailfish, flying fish, sunfish, goldfish, pilotfish, angelfish, char, steelhead

Water Life

whale, porpoise, dolphin, shrimp, crab, starfish, sea anemone, octopus, squid, clam, sea snake, crayfish, lobster, mussel, oyster, seal, sea lion, sea otter, sea horse, walrus, sea urchin, jellyfish, scallop, prawn, ray, skate, beaver, penguin, sea cucumber, sand dollar, coral, barnacle, sea plume, seaweed, sponge, plankton

Man-made Structures Associated With Water

bridge, drawbridge, swing bridge, suspension bridge, pontoon bridge, tunnel, moat, dam, reservoir, irrigation systems, hydroelectric systems, buoy, lighthouse, breakwater, marina, quay, wharf

---

WORKCARD SETS

Nautical Notes

This set of workcards requires the child to recall and name nautical facts.

These cards can be used orally or in a written assignment.

Children may be asked to note or name:

> three rivers
>
> four oceans
>
> five lakes
>
> six fresh-water fish
>
> two sea mammals
>
> four shelled animals
>
> a waterfall
>
> two beaches
>
> three kinds of fishing tackle
>
> five kinds of boats
>
> three sea plants
>
> four pieces of diving gear
>
> a bridge
>
> four kinds of seafood

The numbers can be adapted to the grade level and ability of the children.

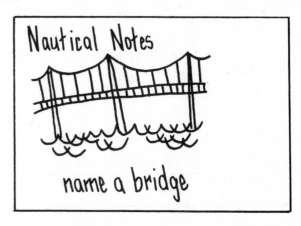

Anchors Aweigh

This set of workcards requires the child to take a card and weigh each of three objects.

The weights are then recorded and graphed in a notebook or on the corresponding WORKSHEET, see page 141.

> five shells, 100 cc of water, 50 cc of sand
>
> seven plastic boats, one piece of drift-wood, 70 cc of water
>
> one starfish, ten shells, one piece of rope
>
> one compass, one long piece of rope, one telescope
>
> one bucket, one shovel, 100 cc of sand
>
> two small rocks, one sea urchin, one crab shell
>
> one swim mask, one snorkel, one flipper
>
> one toy tugboat, one wooden toy car, six shells
>
> 40 cc of water, twelve shells, two small crabs
>
> one piece of driftwood, one liter of water, five small rocks

The differences in weights are noted and the sum of their weights totaled.

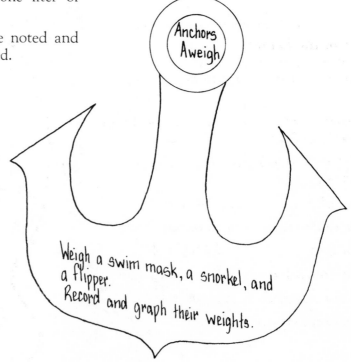

96

If

These cards offer ideas for speaking and writing and can be made using drawings, magazine pictures, or words.

They are useful for promoting discussion within a group or for individual creative writing tasks.

If I had eight arms like an octopus _____

If I had webbed hands and feet _____

If I were as large as a whale _____

If I were a mermaid _____

If I had fins _____

If I were a tadpole _____

If I were a minnow _____

If I were a crab _____

If I were a fisherman _____

If my home were the ocean _____

If I were a tugboat captain _____

If I had a shell like a turtle _____

If I had suction tubes like a starfish _____

Parts of the Whole

The child chooses one of these workcards and names or lists the various parts of each object.

Answers may be spontaneous or found through reading.

The objects mentioned on these workcards could be:

a fish	an octopus
a sailboat	a starfish
a crab	a fishing rod
a submarine	a home aquarium
an ocean liner	a crayfish
a cabin cruiser	a clam

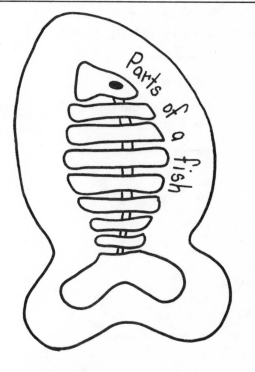

Story Starters

Ideas to promote creative speaking and writing include:

Diving under the water, I opened my eyes to see _____

Cruising the ocean floor in my miniature submarine _____

Reeling in my fishing line, I was surprised to find _____

When I cut open the fish to clean it, I saw _____

We finally arrived at the beach and _____

I was warned of the quicksand, but _____

The ferry pulled away from the wharf, then suddenly _____

We were becalmed for two days when all of a sudden _____

Creeping along the rocks beside the waterfall, we _____

Digging in the sand, I found an old sea chest _____

Reeling around, I saw the pirate's sword flash _____

Swallowed! I'd been swallowed _____

The treasure map led us to _____

I heard a terrific splash, then _____

As the beam from the lighthouse shone on the water _____

Thought Waves

Thought Waves are questions that invite thinking and investigation.

Children respond in group discussions, prepared or recorded talks, or in written or drawn assignments.

What if people had fins instead of feet?

What if people had pincers instead of hands?

Why should people know how to swim?

Why do companies can salmon?

Why is a fish a good pet?

How would we travel if all our roads were canals?

How would we travel if there weren't any bridges?

Why does the Navy have submarines?

Why do we need lighthouses?

Why do we need tugboats?

What if whales became extinct?

Why do cities have aquariums?

Why is water so important?

How could people manage with one-quarter of their usual water supply?

How would you manage in a flood?

Sounders

The teacher makes these phonics workcards in various shapes.

The children choose or are assigned a card and print as many water-related words as they can.

Some sounds and their word possibilities are:

b: bass, beach, bay, bayou, breakers, brook, bog, buoy, billow, babble, barge, bow, beam, bilge, beluga, bridge, barnacles, breakwater

s: shell, sailboat, seal, steamship, sea otter, sand, starfish, swell, salt, sole, snail, sand dollar, sea gull, sailor, shovel, sunglasses, seaweed, stream, sound, salmon, sea horse

o: octopus, otter, ocean, outboard, overboard, oar, ocean liner, outrigger, oyster

f: fish, fins, fishing pole, ferry, fireboat, freighter, fiord, flounder, float

w: whale, water, wade, wharf, waves, whitefish, waterfall, whirlpool, windy, walrus, windward

Versus

Some sorting ideas to use with objects, pictures, or words:

    things that dissolve versus things that do not

    things that float versus things that sink

    things that can breathe under water versus things that cannot

    shelled versus nonshelled

    powerboats versus sailboats

    food from the sea versus food grown on the land

    things on the water versus things under water

    saltwater fish versus fresh-water fish

    tropical versus temperate fish

    pleasure versus commercial craft

Things could be sorted into two buckets, cartons, or hoops; or on sorting boards.

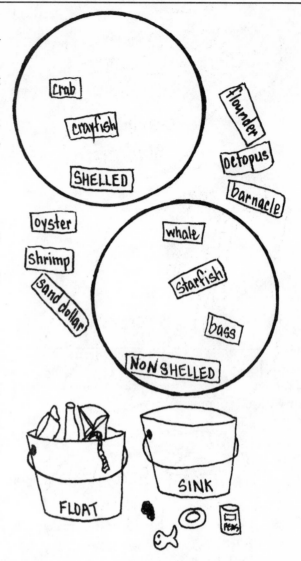

Scramble "riverboat"

Sea Scramble

The cards in this set encourage the children to rearrange the letters of each word in order to make as many new words as possible; instruct the children to see how many new words they can print.

The Sea Scramble cards include the words *seashore*, *waterfall*, *lighthouse*, *ocean liner*, *Coast Guard*, *alligator*, *riverboat*, *steamship*, and *Atlantic Ocean*.

Each Sea Scramble word is listed below with its possible new words.

seashore: sea, or, oar, ease, her, has, sash, rash, ash, see, as, ear, hear, share, hare, shoe, he, she, are, sear, here, horse, hoarse, hearse, soar, shore

waterfall: water, fall, wear, tear, fear, feat, eat, late, fate, rate, ate, teal, tall, wall, fell, tell, well, let, wet, at, fat, flat, rat, alter, falter, after, later, wafer, law, raw, few, flew, raft, war, waft, far, tar, are, flaw, awl, welt

lighthouse: light, sight, house, lit, hit, sit, out, shout, gout, lot, hot, got, shot, sot, let, get, set, the, this, so, those, lose, louse, hose, host, ghost, lost, go, to, high, thigh, sigh, use, tough, slough, though, height, sleigh, eight, tousle, sleight

alligator: all, at, rat, tall, gall, gill, till, rail, tail, oar, goat, gloat, ill, toll, roll, grill, gloat, got, rot, rag, lag, tag, ail, rig, rail, liar, trail

riverboat: rib, rob, tab, at, bat, rat, vat, oar, tore, roar, are, beat, eat, tear, ear, rear, bear, air, rare, bare, tar, bar, boar, roar

steamship: steam, ship, am, tea, team, seam, meat, shame, ham, same, tame, tam, him, his, mast, past, has, mash, smash, mesh, mess, pest, east, peat, heat, seat, eat, aim, map, hip, tip, sip, step, stem, tape, shape, ape, sap, tap, sham, pass, mass, she, he, mate, haste, paste

Atlantic Ocean: at, can, tan, an, a, attic, antic, lance, loin, lion, coin, cane, cone, lace, lane, tot, ton, tone, ten, one, ace, tail, tale, tile, toil, nail, act, cat, coat, loan, alone, lone, talon, talent, can't, in, tint, tent, taint, cent, clean, clan, clot, lot, not, cot, neat, eat, ant, tonic, once, oil, note, tote, talc, to, it, lit, alto, cattle, tin, lint, action

ocean liner: one, lone, cone, alone, on, an, are, care, rail, nail, ail, air, liar, lean, clean, cleaner, clan, cane, lane, rain, crane, ran, can, line, linear, ear, near, leer, clear, recline, oar, in

Coast Guard: roast, goat, oats, coat, cat, at, sat, rat, got, tot, rot, sot, dot, cot, cost, us, gust, rust, dust, crust, soar, gut, cut, rut, dart, star, drag, drug, road, as, gas, gust, cog, cast, cards, car, court, gourd

Lined paper cut into special shapes adds interest to assigned spelling, handwriting, or language activities. For display, the shapes can be outlined with crayons or felt pens or mounted on colored paper.

BOOKLETS

Child-made Booklets

Children may choose or be assigned to complete a booklet on any type of life or activity related to water.

The booklet would contain pictures, or pictures and child-dictated sentences, or child-written reports and illustrations.

The type of booklet would depend upon the ability of the specific child.

Remember that these booklets would be based upon the child's observations, experiences, and on-the-spot discoveries, not on readings or research tasks.

Some ideas for booklets are:

> crawly crabs
>
> fish I saw
>
> the white whale
>
> swimming, swimming, in the swimming pool
>
> all kinds of boats
>
> floaters

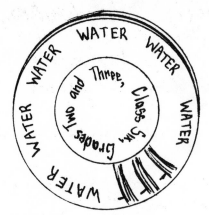

Class-made Booklets
our visit to the aquarium

in the tidal pools

rushing rivers

pond life

swamps

water, water, water!

at _____ lake

fun at the beach

falling water = waterfall

a trip on the ferry

down at the dock

Metal rings are excellent for holding together class booklets. Rings of various diameters can be obtained in stationery stores, and are often cheaper when purchased in large quantities. Other uses for metal rings include holding cards with unit words, arithmetic facts for practice, key words for individual children, and ideas, poems, and finger plays for your easy reference.

Matching Tasks
CUTOUT COLLAGES
Children look through magazines and cut out pictures of things that fall into certain categories.

The pictures are then pasted onto a large piece of paper to make a collage.

Examples of classification categories are:

> things that can swim

> things that can float

> things that can breathe under water

> all types of boats

> things that enable us to cross a body of water

> things seen at the beach

> things found on a boat

THINGS THAT GO TOGETHER
The teacher prepares cards showing things that go together for the children to match on a table, on the floor, or on a pegboard.

Examples of things that go together are:

> a rowboat and an oar

> a sailboat and a sail

> a treasure map and a treasure chest

> a diver and an air tank

> a fisherman and a fishing rod

> a pail and a shovel

> a diving board and a swimming pool

> a tugboat and a barge

> a paddleboat and a wheel

> a motorboat and an outboard engine

> flippers and a mask

> a bathing suit and a towel

> goldfish and a bowl

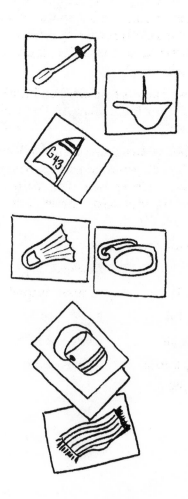

SIMILAR CARDS

The child looks through a set of cards and matches the pairs which are identical.

This task would be more difficult if all the cards contained one object with the differences being in the detailed designs.

CHARTING PAIRS

Children take turns matching identical undersea creatures or plants which the teacher has drawn or cut out and pasted onto a chart.

If the chart is laminated, the children can join the matching pictures with a crayon, and the chart can be wiped clean for later use.

The children should be encouraged to use a left-to-right movement when joining the matching pairs.

RHYMING WORDS

The teacher cuts out or draws pictures of things that rhyme and mounts them on cards for the children to sort (pieces of rubber magnetic tape could be glued to the back of each card).

The teacher cuts out or draws pictures and puts them on a large chart to be used in a group lesson.

The teacher makes a worksheet containing drawings of the rhyming words on which the children either join the things that rhyme, or cut and paste the rhyming pairs together.

Examples of rhyming words are:

boat, coat	bridge, fridge
fish, dish	tunnel, funnel
frog, log	knot, pot
pail, snail	ferry, berry
sand, hand	waves, caves
eel, wheel	

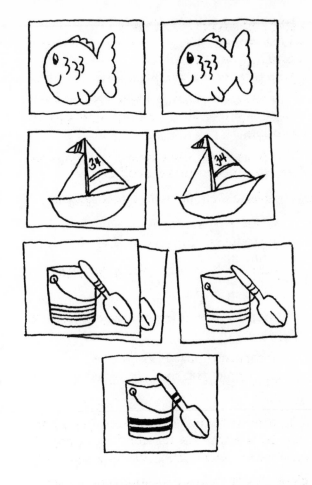

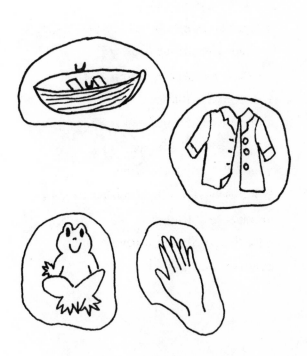

Ordering Tasks

ORDERING CHART

The teacher works with a small group.

The children listen carefully and follow the teacher's directions, such as:

> Draw a line under the smallest seaweed.

> Draw a box around the medium-sized fish.

> Draw a circle above the biggest fish.

The teacher puts more objects in each row or introduces ordinal numbers to increase the difficulty of the concepts.

SEA PACKETS

The teacher provides the children with envelopes, each containing varying sizes of paper sea objects.

The children must place the fish, starfish, boats, whales, or snails in order according to size.

Discarded texts, library books, and magazines are invaluable in the preparation of many activities. The photographs can be used for sorting, classifying, ordering, discussion, and story writing. Or, the pictures can be cut out and mounted forming a booklet to encourage student authors or forming a teacher-made reader suited to the vocabulary of a group or individual.

Directional Tasks
DESCRIPTIVE DIRECTIONS
The teacher works with a small group.

The children listen carefully and they follow the teacher's directions, such as:

Put a circle around the fattest fish.

Draw three lines under the triangular fish.

Draw some seaweed above the smiling octopus.

Draw a starfish in the lower right-hand corner.

Draw a little fish at the left side of the seaweed.

A SCHOOL OF FISH

The teacher works with a group of children.

Eight children are each given a different colored fish and are instructed to stand in a row at the front of the group.

The rest of the children listen carefully, and take turns following the teacher's directions, such as:

Stand in front of the blue fish.

Sit under the red fish.

Clap your hands above the yellow fish.

Stand between the brown fish and the blue fish.

Hop four times behind the purple fish.

Stand beside the black fish.

Floating Pictures

Each child is instructed to find two or three pictures of things that float, such as ships, boats, rafts, fish, whales, beach balls, air mattresses, Styrofoam floaters, surfboards, paddle boards, water skis, driftwood, or lily pads.

Each child then glues his or her pictures onto a large piece of paper to form a widely-spaced collage.

When all the pictures have been glued, a watery blue paint is brushed over the entire paper.

This activity can be done in small groups, or individual floating pictures can be made by each child.

Fishing Fun

A fishing pole with a magnet attached to the string is used.

Cardboard fish, each with a paper clip attached, are used to reinforce various concepts.

The children are to go fishing, following the teacher's directions.

Some ideas for Fishing Fun are:

The child catches three fish, each with a number printed on it, then prints the equation and gives the sum.

The child catches colored fish and sorts them into fishing bags that have the color words printed on them.

The child catches a fish with a phonetic sound on it and must list four words containing that sound.

The child catches a fish that has a story beginning or title on it; he must write the story.

The child catches a fish that has three descriptive words and must write a sentence or short paragraph containing all three words.

Fish are labeled with hundreds, tens, and ones; the child catches three fish and must give the number that they total (for example, if a child catches one fish that says "five ones," one fish that says "two tens," and one fish that says "three hundreds"; the number they total would be 325).

Ships' Logs

INDIVIDUAL LOGS

The children can keep individual logs of their daily activities; listing times, accomplishments, feelings, and personal goals; these logs may be small booklets with one page for each day spent on this unit.

DIARIES

Logs in the form of small diaries may be kept to record at-home or out-of-school events; these develop the children's skill in recording, as well as give the teacher an insight into his or her pupils.

IMAGINARY SHIP'S LOG

The log of an imaginary ship can be kept, as a class or an individual effort, with the children taking the role of the captain and recording the experiences of a voyage.

Water in Motion

The teacher exposes the children to a variety of experiences to help them develop an awareness of the sights, sounds, and movements of water.

These experiences may include films, records, tape recordings, field trips, photography, and experiments with water using a water tank, bathtub, swimming pool, stream, or a running faucet.

After these experiences, the teacher elicits words which describe the action, sights, and sounds of water, for example, squirt, splash, spout, rush, gush, ebb, flow, race, whirl, swirl, billow, surge, swell, ripple, run, meander, drip, swirl, dribble, murmur, babble, gurgle, spurt, ooze, choppy, rolling, wavy, and spray.

The teacher also encourages the children to match the previous descriptive words with examples of moving water, such as river, lake, ocean, waterfall, sluice, course, current, tide, spring, undercurrent, undertow, eddy, whirlpool, surf, breakers, and tidal wave.

These lists are made into a large wall chart and displayed so the children can refer to them when writing stories and poetry, answering questions, or doing projects.

List-a-Fish

There are three players; two taking turns and one acting as the judge.

The two players take turns rolling a die and when each one lands, he must give the name of a fish beginning with the letter indicated.

The judge records (out of view) each fish named in order to prevent repetitions.

If a repetition is made, the player must go back to the beginning.

The winner is the first player to reach the end.

Some examples of fish are: bass, carp, catfish, cod, eel, flounder, halibut, herring, bluefish, mackerel, muskie, perch, pickerel, pipefish, pike, salmon, sardine, smelt, trout, tuna, pilotfish, swordfish, shark, sailfish, marlin, flying fish, sunfish, goldfish, angelfish, char, and steelhead.

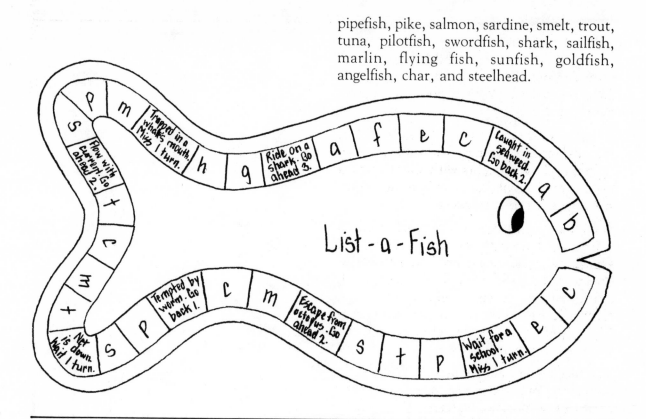

List-a-Fish

Fish Bowl

Children sit in a circle to represent a fish bowl.

One child sits in the middle and hides his or her eyes.

One child sitting in the circle is a fish and says "glub, glub." The child in the center must find him by listening carefully.

The child in the center has three guesses to identify the fish (with young children, "glub, glub" could be repeated after an incorrect guess so that the child in the middle has a better chance of identifying who is making the sounds).

When the fish is identified, he or she then sits in the middle and has a turn to guess.

Ship Ahoy!

Two to four players participate, using a game board, markers, and two dice (one die has the numbers one through six; the other die has the nautical terms *fore*, *aft*, *bow*, *stern*, *port*, *starboard*).

The players take turns rolling the dice and moving accordingly.

If a player lands on a square with stairs, he may move up to the next deck; if he lands on a square with a rope, he must descend to the lower deck.

The winner is the first player to arrive at the captain's cabin.

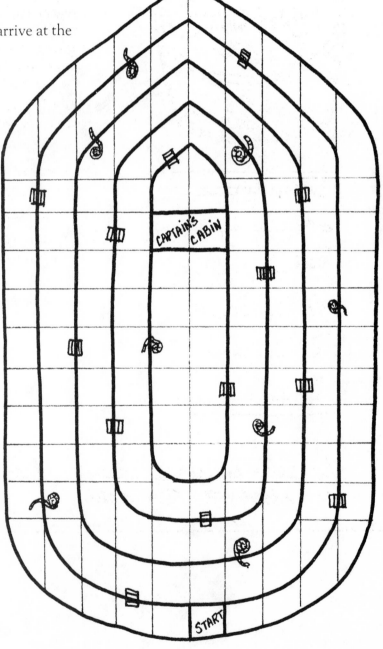

Water Works

A variety of containers are used for water play, such as a large dishpan, a plastic wading pool, a discarded baby bath, or several large plastic buckets.

The children are encouraged to use a variety of objects during free play and in discovery tasks such as those in PROJECTS, pages 116–120. Objects could include: boats (toy or child-made), discarded containers (bleach bottles, milk cartons, soup or juice cans, cottage cheese or margarine tubs, ice-cream buckets), measurement tools such as those used in baking or science experiments, articles found in nature, and articles found around the home and school.

In order to direct the children in their water work, the teacher:

> gives oral instructions
>
> makes and laminates task cards
>
> provides directional lists
>
> provides Venn diagrams to be filled in
>
> provides charts and graphs to be completed

Children are taught to record their findings in a booklet called Water Works.

To renew or arouse interest, food coloring can be added to the water.

Compound Words
INDIVIDUAL LISTS
Using the words *fish*, *boat*, *sea*, or *water*, the teacher displays a word and instructs the children to list as many compound words containing that word as they can.

At the end of a set period of time (a few minutes, an hour, a day, or a week), the word lists are checked and discussed.

A winner might be announced if the teacher feels that competition is of any value.

CLASS LISTS
The teacher prints a word on a chart and instructs the children to take turns listing the compound words.

The compound words are later used in sentences or in a story dictated by the class.

TEAM LISTS
The children are divided into two teams and one person on each team is chosen to be the recorder.

The teacher displays a word and instructs the teams to list as many compound words as possible.

The winning team is the one with the most words.

If the words are recorded on a chalkboard or a large sheet of paper, they will be easily seen and checked by the teacher, the audience, and the opposing team.

> *sea* compounds: seaborne, seacoast, seagoing, seashore, seaweed, seafood, seafloor, seaman, seamark, seaside, seasick, seaward, seaway, seaplane

> *boat* compounds: boatman, rowboat, boatswain, sailboat, tugboat, longboat, iceboat, powerboat, lifeboat, motorboat, houseboat, boathouse, steamboat

> *fish* compounds: sailfish, dogfish, catfish, sunfish, goldfish, starfish, angelfish, fishwife, spadefish, triggerfish, whitefish, fishnet, fishhook, fishbone, fishbowl, fishable, fishtail

water compounds: waterborne, water-
color, watercraft, waterfall, waterfowl,
watermark, waterfront, watermelon,
waterlog, waterspout, waterscape,
waterproof, waterway, waterweed,
watertight, watershed, waterworks,
waterworn, underwater, breakwater

Treasure Hunt

Two to four players with a game board,
markers, dice, and direction cards may play.

Players take turns rolling the dice and
moving accordingly.

As each player moves along, he or she must
answer the arithmetic questions printed on
the spaces or lose a turn.

When a player lands on a space marked
with a treasure chest, he or she chooses and
follows a direction card; for example, if the
card "go to the rowboat" is chosen, the
player moves his or her marker to the space
adjacent to the rowboat.

The player, on his or her next turn, moves
according to the dice.

Row, Row, Row Your Boat

Each child draws and cuts out a little person and prints his or her name on it.

The teacher makes and displays a large paper rowboat in which the children can place their people when they have accomplished a specific task.

This rowboat can be used to indicate:

those capable of reading a list of phonetically spelled words

those successful in an oral arithmetic drill

successful participants in a spelling quiz

completion of assignments

the classroom helpers

improvement in work habits

Several rowboats can be made for group competition.

PROJECTS

Things That Dissolve and Change in Water

THINGS THAT DISSOLVE:
sugar, salt, instant coffee, juice crystals, powdered spices, gelatin powders, baking soda, bubble bath crystals

THINGS THAT CHANGE:
flour, oatmeal, ice cubes, soap, bran, rice, dirt, soda crackers, piece of bread, wallpaper paste, plaster, cement, cardboard, newsprint

Children may experiment individually, in small groups, or a whole class may observe demonstrations.

In any case, the children record their findings, and make graphs or diagrams.

In the case of individual experiments, each child is asked to give an oral report on his or her procedures and findings.

It might be interesting to compare and contrast the effects of running and still water on the above articles.

Float or Sink

A variety of articles may be collected from home, school, or out of doors and tested; the results may be graphed or recorded.

The effects of water displacement can be tested by varying the levels of water in a collection of like jars or bottles.

Children observe and note the following:

Will an empty jar float?

How do the partially filled jars float?

How much water can a jar hold before it will sink?

When you immerse an empty bottle in water, what happens?

Children can test the floatability of the paper boats or rafts they have made in HANDWORK by adding weights, such as paper clips, pennies, beans, nails, or washers, one at a time, and the results may be recorded on graphs.

To observe interesting effects in water, the class may wish to experiment with oils or detergents.

Bridge Construction

Relating to the physical activities of this unit, the children construct bridges to span spaces.

They should work with a variety of materials, including straws and pins; building blocks; balsa wood and glue; plasticene; wood scraps and nails; or cardboard and string.

Several styles of bridges, including ground-supported and suspension bridges, might be created.

Encourage the children to build and evaluate their constructions, with the following ideas in mind:

Which style of bridge is the strongest?

Which construction material is the most suitable?

What is the longest space that can be spanned?

How far can they build before some means of support is needed?

What additional materials are needed to construct a drawbridge or swing bridge?

Aquariums

These are a terrific means of enhancing observation powers, and encouraging discovery and research.

They provide opportunities for measuring, recording, and graphing; and at the same time allow the children to develop responsibility for their care and upkeep.

The class might have a tropical aquarium and a cool water aquarium, or the teacher may have several smaller aquariums set up for the purpose of group studies.

Guppies and platies (both of which are live-bearing fish), goldfish of various types, newts, salamanders, and water plants are all relatively easy to care for and interesting to observe.

Research

The following are topics or questions which the children may find interesting to explore.

What can water move through?

What happens when you mix air and water?

What can propel a boat?

How can water alter the land?

Water: Helpful and Harmful

Water Pollution

Water Safety

A Water Creature

Boats of All Types

Boating Etiquette

River Source to River Mouth

Readings should form the basis for research, but films, filmstrips, field trips, and experiments may enhance findings and add interest to assigned or chosen tasks.

The children might produce drawings, photographs, movies, models, charts, tape recordings, and written accounts to report their research.

Driftwood

Make a collection of assorted driftwood pieces.

It's terrific for creating sea animals, mobiles, and for sanding and varnishing or painting as small gifts.

Interesting rubbings and printings can also be made.

Things You Can Do With Seashells

Make individual or group collections.

Describe them by color, surface texture, size, and shape.

Use feely bags or games to enhance this activity.

Weigh and measure them.

Compare them.

Record the findings.

Classify them according to color, surface texture, size, shape, or weight.

Use clam shells for arithmetic problems involving halves (single shell sections) and wholes (where the two sections of the clam shell remain joined).

Use them as counters.

Make printings and rubbings with them.

Create pictures with them.

Glue them together to form sea animals or other creatures.

Use pipe cleaners, tissue paper, Popsicle sticks, paint, and wire in the constructions.

String them.

Photographic Analysis

Children use cameras to take movies, slides, or prints for their analysis of water.

They may explore several facets of water, deciding which photographs will best illustrate their ideas.

Some possibilities for studies are:

reflections of clouds, plants, animals, buildings, people, and objects on smooth or rippled water surfaces

moods created by the changing appearance of water caused by the weather, the seasons, or the time of day

motions of an ocean, fountain, stream, river, waterfall, lake, or pond

uses of water

Children make photographic displays and presentations using their own captions and commentaries, and possibly some appropriate poetry or music.

These studies develop an awareness and a sensitivity in the children.

These studies also encourage story writing, poetry, drama, music, drawing, and painting.

To set the mood for this unit's studies, cut blue and green crepe paper into long, wavy strips and suspend them from the ceiling. These strips will create a sealike atmosphere in the classroom and will provide a background for the sea creatures which the children will make. Or, attach rows of wavy crepe paper strips along a bulletin board to give a watery effect to your displays.

Wax and Tissue

Children cut fish, undersea plants, air bubbles, divers, sunken ships, and other water objects from various colors of tissue paper.

These are placed between two sheets of wax paper.

The tissue is then sealed into the wax paper by ironing (best results are obtained by placing the ready-to-iron sheets between layers of newspaper and ironing on a low setting).

Before ironing, check to see that there is a border of wax paper as wide as your finger around the outside edges to ensure sealing.

The wax and tissue picture may be framed with colored construction paper and hung on a string or mounted on a window using rolled masking tape on the back of the frame.

Another way of displaying the wax and tissue picture is to cut it into a fish shape or an irregular shape and suspend it near a light source.

Paper Plate Aquariums

Supply the children with paper plates, construction paper, crepe paper, tissue paper, cellophane, thread, needles, glue, and scissors.

Each child uses two paper plates (one whole, and one with the center cut out); the centerless plate has blue or green cellophane attached on the inside to cover the hole.

Painted or decorated cans make useful holders for children's scissors. Simply punch holes around the perimeter of the lid with a can opener and insert the points of the scissors into the holes.

The child uses any of the remaining types of paper to make his or her own aquarium; the aquarium occupants may be glued down or suspended by thread from the edge of the plates.

The two paper plates are stapled together, and may be displayed as aquariums, or as portholes on a submarine or boat.

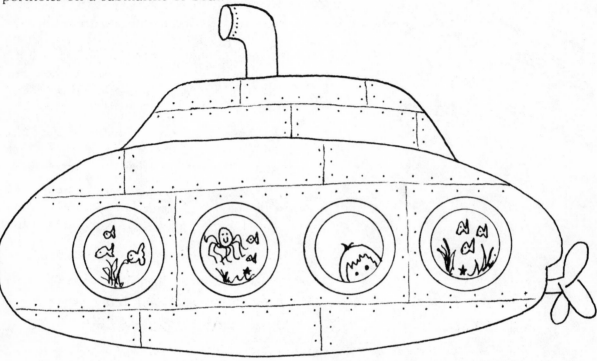

Paper Strip Creatures
FISH

Each child will need three paper strips cut at least 1¼ in. (3 cm) wide; one of which is 12 in. (30 cm) long and the other two are 8 in. (20 cm) long.

Measure two finger spaces from each end of the 12 in. (30 cm) strip and one of the 8 in. (20 cm) strips and make cuts as shown.

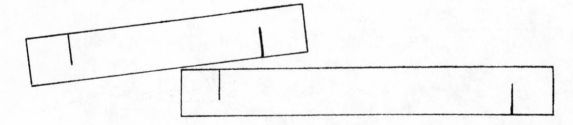

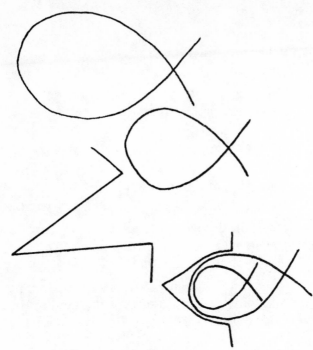

Bring the ends of each piece together interlocking the cuts.

Insert the smaller inside the larger, attaching the rounded fronts together with glue.

The remaining 8 in. (20 cm) piece is folded in the middle and two finger spaces from each end as shown.

The last strip is attached at the top and bottom to form the nose and fins of the fish.

Cut paper pieces may be added to make eyes, or a variety of fins and tails.

These fish may be suspended from or caught in a string or crepe paper net.

String nets can be suspended from the ceiling or along a wall forming an unusual method for displaying handwork or storing materials. Labeled clothespins could hold work to be taken home. Also, children could be responsible for pinning or stringing their good work along the net for display.

OCTOPUS

Each child will need four paper strips cut at least 1¼ in. (3 cm) wide, and 24 in. (60 cm) long.

Fold each strip into thirds, and staple each strip together at the folds to form a body part and two tentacles.

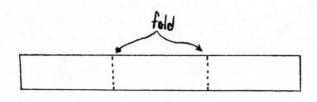

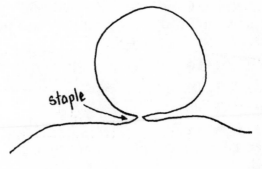

The body sections are placed inside each other at different angles and stapled or glued in place.

Paper eyes may be added and the tentacles may be curled or accordion pleated.

SNAIL
Each child will need three paper strips at least 1¼ in. (3 cm) wide, and 12 in. (30 cm), 8 in. (20 cm), and 6 in. (15 cm) in length.

Both the 6 in. (15 cm) and 8 in. (20 cm) strips are folded and glued to form circles; the smaller is placed inside the larger and attached at the bottom.

The 12 in. (30 cm) strip is attached at its midpoint to the bottom of the circles; the front of the strip is then curled and glued to form a circular head; the back of the strip is accordion folded to form the foot.

Feelers, eyes, and mouth may be added.

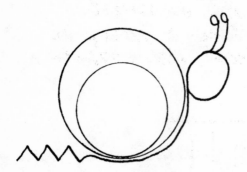

Fish
SCALY FISH
A large fish shape is cut from construction paper and colorful paper circles about 1¼ in. (3 cm) in diameter are overlapped and glued on to form scales, starting at the tail and working up to the gill line.

A large mouth can be drawn and one circle glued in place for an eye.

If desired, the fish can be mounted on colored paper and additional circles glued on to form bubbles.

PAPER BAG FISH
Each child will need a paper lunch bag.

The paper bag is stuffed two-thirds full with crumpled newspaper and the open end is gathered and tied with string to form the tail.

The bottom or flat end forms the face.

Paper facial features and fins are added after the fish is painted.

WALLPAPER FISH
Each child traces and cuts two wallpaper circles.

Onto the wrong side of one circle the child pastes two triangular fins and a fancy tail cut from construction paper.

The other circle is then pasted on with the wrong sides together.

A smiling mouth and wide eyes can then be added.

Because these fish are two-sided, they can be hung effectively.

You may choose to make one or several crepe paper nets by cutting a package of crepe paper. Simply remove the wrapper and cut as shown:

Keeping the crepe paper flat, carefully unfold it one section at a time.

CONSTRUCTION PAPER FISH

This mobile-like fish is made of two or more parts, each part fitting inside the other; the larger the first fish is made, the more parts this mobile will have, since each smaller fish is made from the discarded midsection of the larger fish.

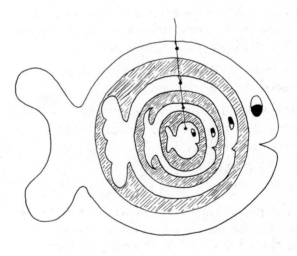

The child begins by drawing and cutting out a large circular or oval fish that has a triangular tail.

The midsection of this fish is then cut out, leaving a hole in the middle of the body.

This process is continued, and then the fish are strung consecutively inside each other.

Boats

FLOATABLE DISCARDS

Children use paper plates, paper cups, milk cartons (cut in half lengthwise), or one-half of an egg carton to make boats.

Children use different types of materials and scraps to create a variety of boats.

The teacher allows the children to create their own original boats or gives them some direction as to the type of boat to build, such as sailboats, funny boats, or passenger boats.

Although you wish to provide the children with a wide variety of materials, it is often difficult to make these easily accessible. Prestrung needles, pins, thumbtacks, and fine wire can be stuck into bulletin board. Pipe cleaners, paper scraps, corks, wooden dowels, Popsicle sticks, toothpicks, and straws are neatly stored and ready for use when kept in large cloth pockets or brown paper envelopes.

FLAT PAPER BOATS

Using a square piece of origami or brightly colored paper, fold opposite corners together to form a triangle.

Then fold the open edges up to the middle of the folded edge as shown, with the bottom flap behind.

Lastly, fold a single side of the boat's hull back, turning it inside out.

If you begin by folding the colored sides of the origami paper together, the sails will be white and the hull colored.

If the white sides are folded together, the sails will be colored and the hull white.

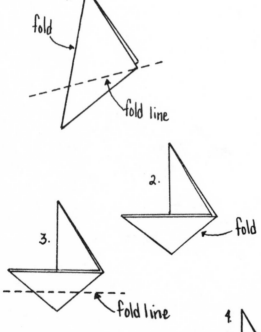

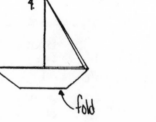

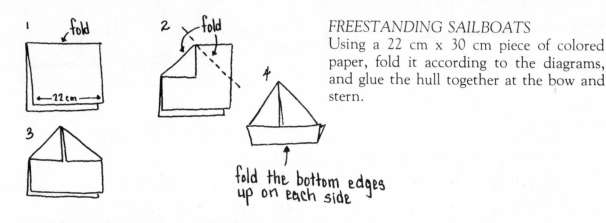

Using a 22 cm x 30 cm piece of colored paper, fold it according to the diagrams, and glue the hull together at the bow and stern.

fold the bottom edges up on each side

Clay or Clay-Dough Sea Creatures
For clay-dough recipe see page 77.

SEA SNAIL
The child rolls two lumps of clay into ropes.

One rope is wound into a flat coil to form the body of the snail.

The coil body is placed in an upright position on the midsection of the second rope.

The front section of the second rope is curved up around the body and then rolled forward to form the head; the tail section can be left flat, or pinched and pleated to form the foot.

Two small antennae may be securely attached.

STARFISH
Using six small lumps of clay, the child makes one flattened ball for the body, and five rounded, triangular pieces for the legs.

Children use their imaginations to find materials with which to texture the starfish.

Some of the legs may be curved or upturned.

OCTOPUS
Using one large lump and eight smaller lumps of clay, the child makes a round ball to form the head and eight ropes to form the tentacles.

The tentacles are securely attached to the bottom of the head and may be curved into flowing arms.

To avoid breakage during firing in a kiln or baking in an oven, all body parts must be fairly thick and be securely attached and blended.

After firing or baking, the sea creatures can be painted and then glazed or shellacked.

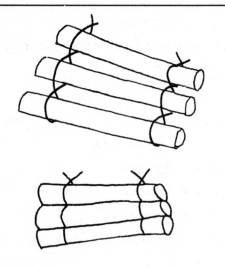

Stick or Balsa Rafts
Child may use small sticks, twigs, or rounded balsa wood pieces to form the base of his or her raft.

Pieces of wood may be glued together with bondfast glue or strung together with string as shown.

A wooden or straw mast may be added and a fabric, tissue, or crepe paper sail attached.

The child may choose to make a pilot for his or her raft.

Children use their rafts during water experimentation.

Hole Punch Fish
The child draws and cuts out a fish shape from light cardboard.

Using hole punches of differing sizes, the child punches holes into the fish to form some kind of a pattern.

The fish can then be used as a printing stamp or as a cutout for spatter painting.

Plasticene Wash Pictures
The child makes an undersea picture by pressing very small amounts of plasticene onto a piece of heavy drawing paper.

When the picture is complete, a thin wash is brushed over the entire paper.

For added effects, two or more colors of plasticene may be used.

Wax Resists
The child makes an undersea picture using crayons, making sure he presses heavily and uses vivid colors.

The child leaves the background of his picture free of color so that a thin blue or green wash may be brushed over the entire paper.

PHYSICAL ACTIVITIES

Bridges

Encourage the children to build bridges by bending and stretching their bodies.

Working alone, in pairs, or in threes, they span spaces, objects, and other children.

They should travel through and over the bridges; they may also roll objects under them.

Have them employ small equipment, such as benches, hoops, balls, chairs, and ropes in their bridge building.

Bridges can be made on the floor, on mats, and against walls.

Give instructions, such as:

Roll the ball; run and make a bridge for the ball to go through.

Make a bridge using two hands and two feet.

Make a bridge over the bench.

Make the lowest bridge you can.

Make a bridge against the wall.

Use a hoop in your bridge.

Travel over and under the chair; then make a bridge over it.

Using as many different ways as you can, travel through your partner's bridge.

Make a bridge for your partner to travel over.

Make a bridge with three children; count the places you could travel through.

Water Orientation

Children need many activities to help them discover and develop their abilities in the water.

It is most important that you give assistance and encouragement.

Safety rules should be stressed and adhered to at all times.

PLAYING IN THE WATER
Encourage the children to:

wade or jump into the water with you

bounce in the water

run in the water

follow the leader

play ring-around-the-rosie

play catch with balls and rings

play tag games

blow bubbles in the water

hold their breath underwater

sit and kneel underwater

open their eyes underwater

bob in and out of hoops

retrieve rings from under the water

FLOATING, GLIDING, AND KICKING
Allow the children to discover their buoyancy through:

using a kick board to ease their floating, gliding, and kicking

floating on their fronts

floating on their backs

creating shapes while floating

gliding on their fronts by pushing off

gliding on their backs by pushing off

kicking while being supported

kicking to propel themselves

turning

somersaulting

treading water

129

Tote bags are a necessity for holding swimsuits and towels. Simple drawstring cloth bags can be easily sewn by classroom mothers or by the children themselves. In the classroom, these bags are handy for storing gym clothing, or even the children's school supplies.

WORKSHEETS

Pages 131, 132

Fill-ins The teacher prints incomplete arithmetic equations or phonetically spelled words on the paper. This may be done before the mimeo is duplicated, or afterwards to allow for individual differences.

Page 133

Sailing, Sailing The children complete this place value sheet by filling in the numbers and drawings, as shown in sailboat number 43.

Page 134

Boats The children look across and down to find the names of the hidden boats. They should circle the names as they find them, as well as cross them out on the word list.

Page 135

What Am I? The children color by number to find the whale.

Page 136

Above, Below This is a page to be used for sorting. Small pictures can be drawn and labeled or cut out and pasted on. In addition, names of animals, articles, and people can be printed in the appropriate places.

Page 137

Seashells The children count, color, and mark the shells according to instructions.

Page 138

The Fisherman Working with ordinals, the children follow the directions given.

Page 139

Fish The children are asked to differentiate fish possessing a variety of characteristics.

Page 140

Dot-to-Dot The children count by two, in order to join the dots and discover this sea creature.

Page 141

Anchors Aweigh The children use this sheet to complete their recording and graphing. See WORKCARD SETS, page 96.

Page 142

Maze The children must help the little sailor through the waves to safety ashore. They may not cross any solid lines.

Page 143

Crossword Puzzle The children complete this puzzle by printing the names of the objects pictured. The answers to the puzzle are: Across: 5. starfish, 6. sail, 7. bridge, 8. canoe, 9. propeller. Down: 1. waterfall, 2. oar, 3. pail, 4. whale, 6. submarine, 10. pool, 11. raft.

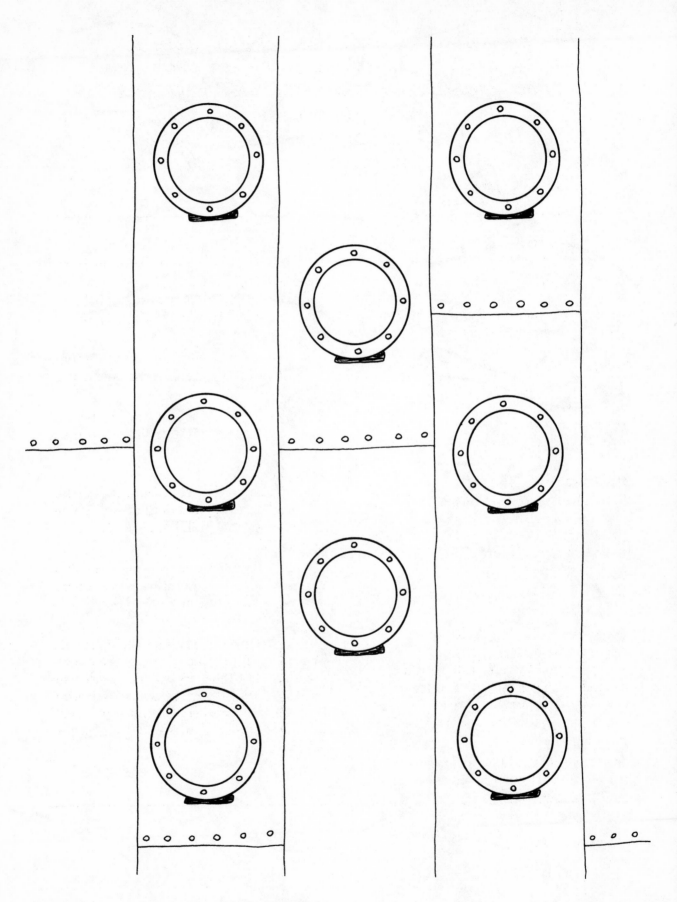

132

Sailing, Sailing

Place Value

BOATS

WORD SEARCH - Look across and down.

barge
canoe
catamaran
dinghy
ferry
freighter
houseboat
Hovercraft
kayak

liner
motorboat
outrigger
raft
rowboat
sailboat
scull
ship

tanker
trawler
tug
yacht

1 = orange   3 = blue
2 = yellow   4 = green

What am I?
Follow the code and color
me to find out.

135

On

Over

Above

Below

Under

In

Seashells

How many large shells?
How many small shells?
How many shells are there in total?

Color three shells green.
Color one shell red.
Color four shells orange.
Color two shells brown.

How many shells are not colored?
Place an X on those shells.

The Fisherman!

How many fish has
this boy caught?
_____

Put an X on the third fish.
Put a △ above the sixth fish.
Put a ○ under the tenth fish.
Put a □ beside the first fish.

Color the eighth fish orange.
Color the eleventh fish red.
Color the ninth fish blue.
Color the fourth fish green.
Color the seventh fish purple.
Color the fifth fish yellow.

Which fish are not
marked or colored?
_____ and _____

Fish

How many fish are there in total?
How many fish are striped?
How many fish are spotted?
How many are fat?
How many are thin?
How many are large?
How many are smaller fish?
How many of the fish look happy?
How many fish are swimming to the right?
How many are swimming to the left?
How many fish have rounded fins?
How many fish have scalloped tails?
How many are looking up?
How many fish are looking down?

Count by two.

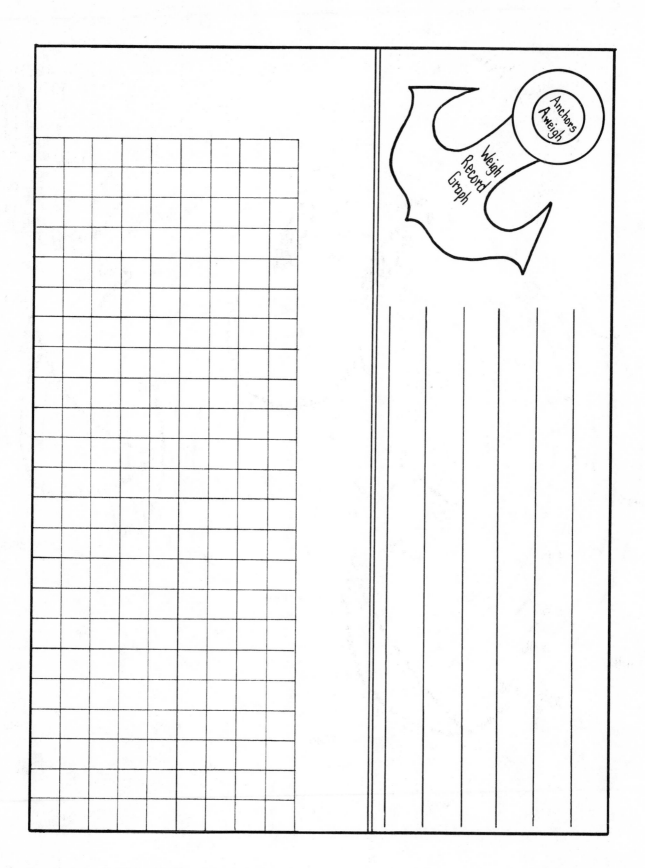

MAZE

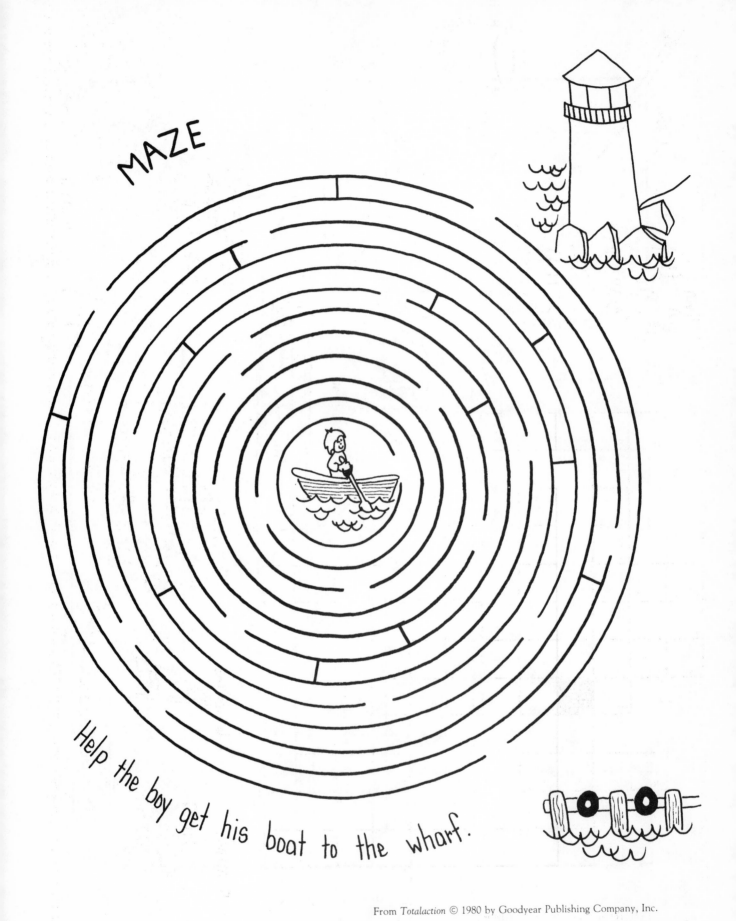

Help the boy get his boat to the wharf.

2 down

3 down

6 down

10 down

11 down

1 down

4 down

Crossword Puzzle

9 across

7 across

6 across
P 73

8 across

5 across